About the Author

Jean was born in South Shields and is very proud to be a Geordie. When she was two years old the family moved to Richmond in Yorkshire, where her father was Borough Electrical Engineer.

She had a wonderful childhood and after passing the scholarship she went to Richmond High School.

In 1943 she was selected to represent the children of Richmond in a broadcast to America called Bridgebuilders.

In 1945 she went to Bingley to train as a teacher. After qualifying, she taught in Darlington Catterick Camp, Richmond, before going as a teacher with the RAF.

After marrying, she and Ken moved to St Annes-on-Sea. She taught juniors until retiring in 1984, then enjoyed playing golf at many of the magnificent courses in Lancashire.

Dedication

I would like to dedicate my book to the RAF personnel I met during my tours, especially those in RAF Abyad, Egypt.
And also to my husband, friends at Old Links Golf Club, who supported and encouraged me to write this book.

Jean Hood

A Mistress Abroad

AUSTIN MACAULEY
PUBLISHERS LTD.

A CIP catalogue record for this title is available from the British Library.

ISBN 978 1 78455 503 0 (Paperback)
ISBN 978 1 78455 505 4 (Hardback)

www.austinmacauley.com

First Published (2015)
Austin Macauley Publishers Ltd.
25 Canada Square
Canary Wharf
London
E14 5LB

Printed and bound in Great Britain

"You are going abroad for a holiday."

"I am going abroad but I'm going to work."

The fortune teller looked at my palm then into my eyes, "Well it will seem like a holiday" and she was right."

I never go to fortune tellers, I prefer to let life take its course, but this was a special day as the cricket club were trying to raise money. The fete had the usual attractions including a lady from the nearby town who had the reputation of being good at predicting the future. She was elderly and as she sat there in her long black coat and old fashioned hat she exuded an air of knowledge, so perhaps she knew something and working abroad would be an enjoyable experience.

I had applied for a teaching job with the RAF teaching the children of RAF personnel. I had an interview at Air Ministry in London with two RAF officers. I had applied in the usual way after reading an advert in *Teachers World.* I had references from my past heads, the mayor of the town and from an army colonel who was in the Education Corps.

One of my references was the manager of the local bank. One lunch time when I arrived home my mother said the bank manager wanted to see me immediately but she didn't know why. I went to the bank and the lady behind the counter said I had to go into Mr Thompson's office he was expecting me.

I went in; he looked at me and said I could go. I asked why he wanted to see me and he said the Air Ministry had sent a form for him to fill in and one of the questions was, "When did you last see the applicant?"

"I can now put today," he said.

As all my references were good it was up to me to perform well at my interview. The Air Ministry had paid for my accommodation and train fare so I went to London with a friend and we halved the cost, we enjoyed shopping and a show and I must have done well because I got the job.

Air Ministry again called me to London after my medical to discuss conditions in Egypt and answer any queries I might have, again it was at their expense so my friend and I enjoyed another few days sampling the delights of the Capital.

I had my medical at RAF Catterick. I was examined by a squadron leader who passed me fit for service abroad and immediately gave me my first injections TABT for tetanus and typhoid. Various other vaccinations were given at various times until April 1953 when I was ready to leave on my big adventure. But first I had to leave family and friends.

As it happened two friends were getting married the day I left so after the reception we all went to catch the train to London. Goodbyes seemed much easier with so any people around and the married couple. I got into the carriage and we were all covered in confetti.

We set off and the occupants of the carriage gave us peculiar looks until eventually one person looked at Mike and said, "Well which one have you married?"

I left them quickly in London; they were going to Switzerland for a honeymoon.

I was going to Woking to stay with a school friend. The next day I arrived at RAF Hendon to meet fellow travellers and make my first flight in a York aeroplane.

The passengers were service personnel wearing uniforms and I was seated next to a flight lieutenant who was obviously a pilot as he had 'wings' and medals on his chest. He sat and fidgeted, felt under his seat and looked around so I asked him what he had lost and could I help him find it. He was looking for the parachute! He didn't like being driven by someone else and was looking for his escape in case we crashed. That certainly helped to give me confidence.

We stopped at Malta to refuel and had a meal of egg and chips; I found this standard fare at all RAF stopping places and then once again took to the air just as it was getting dark. I could see sparks flying out of the engines and I felt like the character in the song that would rather die than complain. But the test pilot next to me assured me it was usual, so I settled back and tried to sleep until we landed at Fayid, mid-morning.

As I stepped off the plane a P/O stepped forward, introduced himself and said he had transport to my camp and he would look after me and help to get me settled in. We drove to Abyad and he escorted me to the teachers' quarters.

As it was Easter all the other teachers were on holiday in Cyprus so I would be on my own until they returned in another week. Our quarters consisted of along low building set in the WAAF compound but quite a way from their buildings. The teachers had their own gate and the whole area was behind barbed wire and sacking. At our entrance there was a security light and of course men were not allowed passed it. John took me to my room and said he would let me freshen up then would meet me in the bar in the Officers' Mess and he'd explain anything I wanted to know.

The teachers' quarters building, my home for the next three years consisted of six rooms with a veranda all round and each room had two doors which opened on to the front veranda and the back to give a through breeze. At the end of the rooms was a passage with another room beyond which had a bath and a washbasin and a separate toilet. The toilet was a chemical one and my first thought was I'm not going to use that. I decided I would 'wait' until I got to the officer's mess and use the toilet there. I washed and changed then went to meet John in the bar.

As it was about 11.45 he was the only one there and after he had ordered a drink I asked where the cloakroom was and he showed me. To my horror that toilet was even worse, it was a bucket with a plank across. As nature was calling very strongly by now I had to use it.

When I returned to the bar it was starting to fill up as the men came in from work. They worked mornings only, because of the heat so they all came to the bar to get a drink. I didn't realise it at the time but when a new female arrived it was quite a novelty as they liked to see her. I was introduced to so many people then John took me to the dining room where I had to sign in as the cost of my meals would go on my mess bill which I had to pay at the end of the month.

He had already organised my book at the bar where any drinks, writing material, cigarettes and cinema tickets would be entered and added to my mess bill.

During the afternoon people usually went to the 'beach.' This was at the edge of the Great Bitter Lake where clubs had been built. There was a club for officers, sergeants and other ranks, a sailing club for all ranks and a Greek club.

Buses went from the camp, through Fayid village to the lakeside. On the way it crossed the Sweet Water canal where the rubbish and dirt made it anything but sweet. We were told that anyone falling into this water would be given 24 terribly painful injections and even then probably die but that it obviously only happened to Europeans as the Egyptian children played happily on its banks.

But that first afternoon I rested then met John for dinner and adjourned to the bar for the evening.

Once again I was introduced to many people, mainly friends of John but as I was tired I left early and went to bed.

Once I had been accepted by the RAF for service overseas I was sent a book called 'Health Hints in Warm Climates.' It was obviously a pamphlet sent to all personnel during the North African campaign in Second World War. It explained how cold the desert could be at night and how to keep warm. I hadn't taken much notice of it as I didn't think I'd be sleeping under the African stars but one item took my interest.

Apparently snakes don't like the cold at night and would find a warm hole such as boots so before putting them on one had to give them a good shake just to make certain they were empty and had no welcome lodgers.

As I went to bed, alone in the block I remembered the article about snakes and carefully pulled the blanket and sheet back to make certain everything was alright and no unwelcome visitor lurked in my bed. I felt very stupid but relieved when I found nothing so after reading for a while I put out the light and settled to sleep.

I was just dropping off when I heard a rattling on the veranda outside my room. As I listened the noise seemed to come nearer and I knew it was at the window. I heard nothing else but this soft rattle and as I listened I was aware it was in the room and slithering toward the bed. I couldn't move, but when it leapt on my bed I screamed, switched on the light and saw on my bedspread a cat with a bell on its collar, this was the rattle I heard.

The cat quite oblivious of the panic it had caused began to purr and roll on the bed. I found out later it belonged to one of the teachers on holiday and I was in her room. She was being posted to Kabrit and would take the cat with her on her return. Pet cats had to be belled as there were so many wild ones around the camp that every so often there was a purge and any cats roaming without a bell were shot.

Next morning I showered, had breakfast in the mess and returned to my quarters. I sat outside in the sunshine to try to get a tan as I stood out like a sore thumb among all the suntanned people. I was white, chalk white, a 'moon woman' and the sooner I got 'my knees brown' the happier I would be. Osman brought me a cup of tea and I settled down with a book.

Osman was our bearer and lived in Fayid village just across the road from the camp. He had to have a pass to get into work and I suppose he had a mainly easy job looking after half a dozen teachers. He cleaned our rooms, collected our washing to take to the Dhobi-Wash-Laundry and made tea and coffee for us. He hadn't always worked for women and the little English he spoke was flavoured with some quite earthy words which always sounded peculiar because he was always so polite.

As I sat, getting warm and a little bored a car drew up to the gate and a Flight Lieutenant I had met the previous day got out and called me over. He wondered if I would like to go out that night to the Officers Club at Fayid for dinner or dancing and I was delighted to accept so we arranged to meet in the bar.

All the vehicles on camp belonged to the forces. I think the only person who had a car of his own was the doctor but anyone else who wanted transport rang up for a taxi. Taxis were only allowed to the main gate, they couldn't come on to the camp and taxi firms had been vetted for security reasons.

I had only one case with me as my luggage was arriving by boat eventually but I had packed a decent dress and I had a lovely evening at the Officers Cub. The food was good, the wine cold and delicious and the band played good and we danced and dined but not under the stars as it was still quite cool in April. We came home by taxi and arranged to meet again. Well as we both lived on the same camp and ate in the same mess hall we would obviously be meeting again but I took it to mean we would become an item.

And the next night after meeting in the bar dining together and having coffee we decided we would go to the Officers' Club on the camp.

This was a separate building just over the barbed wire from the teacher's compound but still within the RAF Abyad camp. It consisted of a room with bar and piano and dart board and a small restaurant and kitchen. It was quite nice to have a meal there instead of the mess and often the officers brought pork or steaks from Kenya or Cyprus and had them cooked at the club. As we had already eaten we went for a drink and a crowd of us played darts. I don't think I had ever thrown a dart before that time but it was great fun and in time I became quite proficient and enjoyed it.

But that night I was a real beginner. We divided into teams; we played, had a drink and laughed a lot. One of the men seemed a little different from the others. For a start off they all called him sir and he seemed to be directing operations. He flirted with me but it was very light-hearted and I asked him who he was and he replied he was a pilot officer. Now even I knew that squadron leaders and flight lieutenants didn't call a P.O. sir and anyway, as I told him he was too old to be such a low rank. Behind him one of the fellows laid four fingers over his sleeve but I was unaware of RAF ranks and didn't realise that they were trying to tell me he was a Group Captain.

At the end of the evening he offered to escort me 'home' and the others stood back, even Wes, so I left with him.

He asked me to go to his quarters for a night cap, apparently he was living in the CO's house but I declined and left him at the security light outside our quarters.

Next day when I walked into the mess at lunch time I was besieged by friends from the night before asking what had happened, and when I told them I think they were quite disappointed. Apparently last night had been his farewell as he was posted to the U.K. and had already left.

Whilst I waited for the teachers to return and work to begin term I spent my time very pleasantly. After a late breakfast, I read, wandered around camp and after lunch I caught the bus to the beach. The bus was a converted truck with no glass in the windows and painted blue and white. They were run by the RAF and travelled between camps around the Great Bitter Lake. The bus to the beach travelled through the shopping centre at Fayid, passing the various beach clubs to the Officers' Club.

The club had changing rooms, hairdressers and of course a large restaurant and dance area and very good band.

The beach was good but the water at the edge was wormy and a bit grubby. To improve the swimming a causeway had been erected to a barge which was moored about 100 yards from the edge of the lake. There the water was deep and cool and it was so refreshing to cool off after the heat.

On returning to camp after a shower and rest it was over to the mess for dinner and then either we would sit on the lawn outside the mess or go to the open air cinema or even go to the little officers club and play darts! If I had been paying for this it would have cost pounds.

There was only one slight cloud on the horizon; it was about 10 a.m. every morning when the 'Lavender wagon' arrived. It would come to the compound like a great petrol tanker, the RAF driver would stop and two people would enter our quarters. Two armed guards stood shot gun at the back of the wagon with guns at the ready although what they were guarding was hard to imagine. The men who came in collected the chemical toilet and emptied it in the wagon. The smell was awful and the flies followed it everywhere. When the tanker was full I understand it was driven into the desert and dumped.

Somewhere in Egypt there must be some of the most fertile land just waiting to produce lush crops. I wonder if the fellows who were on the wagon were on jankers, it must have been one of the most unpleasant but essential jobs in the RAF.

The Easter holiday ended and normal work resumed. The teachers on holiday In Cyprus returned and welcomed me. One of them the owner of the cat, prepared to go to her new posting in Kabrit at the southern end of the Bitter Lake. The other teacher a Welsh girl called Olwen quizzed me about people I had met and took me over to the mess where I met my headmaster who had returned from holiday in the UK where he had a wife and grown up children. He had previously worked for the Egyptian government in a Cairo school but as relations had become a little soured he had left but been recruited to work in RAF schools in the Canal Zone.

He was a tall, handsome, grey-haired gentleman with a quiet authority and I rarely saw him lose his temper or raise his voice. Olwen on the other hand was a voluptuous dark eyed lady with short black hair and very 'plummy' voice. She played the piano for school assemblies and after the hymn when the class said the Lord's prayer everyone waited for the sound of a match striking as she lit a cigarette. She had been doing this for so long that no one thought of asking her to stop.

I asked the Head Mr Strong which class I would be taking and he told me the first class of five years old. I had been trained to teach juniors aged 7 – 11; I had only ever taught juniors and the thought of having the admission class appalled me.

I told him I had never taught five year olds and he said not to worry an infant teacher was coming out in a month's time so surely I could manage until then.

So for a month I kept them occupied drawing and playing and telling stories until the new teacher turned up. I greeted her with "Thank goodness an infant teacher has arrived."

She replied "I'm not infant, I'm top juniors."

When Mr Strong heard, he told us that as there were so many infants we could split the class between us!

There could always be a problem with RAF schools that many children in the same age group could arrive at once. Sometimes classes would be large then suddenly many fathers were moved and classes diminished. There was also the problem of children being moved so often that they missed the basics and very bright children would be behind in the basic subjects of reading and arithmetic.

I couldn't have young children playing all day, so I went to the small library in the Education Section and found, The Beacon Manual. It was fantastic it described in great detail how to teach reading using both phonetics and word recognition. It had sets of books and the accompanying library books but it didn't have flash cards for either words or sounds so I made them. The other teacher, Maggie, and I, got on well together and had great fun with the sounds and soon had our friends in the mess doing 'f' for feather or blowing imaginary feathers into the air to get the sound.

I'm afraid the children had very formal lessons but the progress they made in a very short time was very rewarding. As soon as they reached a certain stage they were moved on and we really felt we were doing a good job. Of course the children still had their play time and they seemed very happy. We had some very bright children. I was talking one day about vowels and how all words had vowels except for little words like my and by and one little chap piped up "Rhythm doesn't have a vowel." I had to think for a couple of seconds before explaining that 'y sometimes takes the place of a vowel. I wonder where he is and what he is doing now!

1953 was Coronation year and up and down the Canal Zone Coronation Balls were held. Every station had a theme and Abyad sent to Cairo for a contractor to bring in carpets which were draped on the lawn and road outside the mess to form what I suppose was meant to represent an Arabian factory. They formed 'walls' but there were gaps to allow the breeze to come through.

Tables and chairs were on the lawn, dancing in the road and the buffet and drinks were inside in the dining room and bar. Everything was free (except champagne) and a percentage of salary according to rank was added to the mess bill to pay for it. Teachers were ranked as lieutenants and lieutenants. It was a wonderful evening. I suppose having free drinks, with everyone making sure they got value for their contribution helped to make the ball a success. It finished in the early hours of the morning and then the contractors moved in to take down the carpets and then they moved out.

Maggie and I were invited to the Coronation Ball at Fanara although I hadn't met the fellow who had invited me, I think he wanted a partner and asked Maggie's escort if she could find a friend.

So we got on the special bus taking all the guests to the ball. We were the only two women on our own. Behind us were two Squadron Leaders who wondered if we had invitations and obviously didn't want us to be humiliated by being refused admission, so they asked if we had invitations. We replied we hadn't.

"But you have to show your invitation so you can be announced. Did you not know that?"

We replied "No we thought if you wanted to go to a dance you could, just like you do in UK."

They explained that things were different out here but we could go with them on their invitation. Of course we were met off the bus by an escort and given our dance cards and a pencil just like in the olden days. Our two squadron leaders, the two Tommies as we called them saw the joke and wrote their names on our dance cards to show there was no ill feeling.

It was just as well they did as my escort turned out to be the organiser of the ball and I saw very little of him during the whole evening. But he had certainly done a good job on the décor. It was made to represent a London Underground station and they had made cubicle boxes and London Underground had kindly sent loads of posters and the effect although not authentic was fun and reminded people of London.

RAF stations all over the Middle East celebrated the Coronation in different ways. I don't know how true it was but I heard Habbaniyah in Iraq turned a room upside down putting chairs and tables on the ceiling and lights sticking up from the floor.

We went to another Coronation Ball at Kabrit. Again we had to have a proper invitation and be announced but we weren't given dance cards and pencils so it was just like a normal dance.

Of course the dances were formal, the men wore mess uniforms and the ladies all wore long dresses which trailed in the sand and got a little bit grubby around the hem line. As it was warm there was no need for a fur coat and the favourite wrap over on evening dress was a Crusader cape.

These were bought in Jordan and were made in velvet in the most brilliant colours, red, blue, green and black. They were decorated with gold braiding and vivid embroidery which I suppose represented jewels. They could be bought with little skull caps and Dolly Varden bags in the same material and decoration.

I say there was no use for fur coats but I did take my beaver lamb coat and after my first leave, it was useful in winter when nights got rather cold and I would put it on my bed on very cold nights.

When I returned to England I had it cleaned and when I collected it, the cleaner said he had never seen so much sand whatever had I been doing with it.

Wes had been invited to a dance at Deversoir, a RAF camp north of Abyci. About eight people were going from our station so Wes applied and requested two cars to take us there. Cars were not allowed to travel singly in case they broke down and officers had to draw guns from the armoury for the journey. In the past cars had been stopped by Egyptian militants and the drivers attacked so these procedures had been ordered for safety reasons. It was quite exciting to be driven in a car with two men in the front with guns at the ready.

Well it was exciting until the engine of our car began to stutter and we slowed down. We didn't dare to stop the accompanying car in front just sped off leaving us to our fate. We timed a check point a few miles ahead and we managed to keep going until we reached it. The car with us had stopped at the check point and alerted them of our predicament but had we completely stopped, rescue might have arrived too late. Still we were going, alive and thoroughly enjoyed the dance.

Abyad had a thriving Amateur Dramatic Society. Their first play was 'See How They Run' in 1949 and every year they put on a production in the theatre in the camp.

When I arrived in 1953 they had already performed 'Little Lambs Eat Ivy' and I was just in time to audition for 'We Proudly Present' and later in the year the company put in 'Night Must Fall.'

I had always been keen on amateur dramatics at School College and later when I started teaching at my home town of Richmond. I acted the part of Mrs Terence, the chairlady at Richmond's production of 'Night Must Fall.' I was also a member of the Signals Theatre at Catterick Camp (later the Cary Theatre) after the GOC Catterick Garrison General Gary. In that production I played Olivia so when Abyad decided to produce 'Night Must Fall' I really felt I knew the play backwards. Once again I was given the part of Olivia.

To return to the Signals Theatre, the GOC General Gary was a very keen thespian and somehow many of the acting fraternity who had to do National Service found themselves at Catterick camp.

I suppose they did the usual parades etc. associated with military life but they seemed to spend most of their time at the Theatre. They seemed to put on a production every six weeks which was well supported by the soldiers and the civilians who worked there and people from Richmond. It was so successful that it featured in a BBC Home Service programme called 'These Our Actors' which broadcast an excerpt from 'The Man Who Came to Dinner.' This has a cast of over 40 so you can see it was a very thriving Amateur Dramatic Company.

'The Man Who Came to Dinner' was the General himself and it was the third time he had played the part. The play this time was produced by L.C. Donald Adams who had worked for the BBC was a member of the Old Vic in Bristol and later of the D'Oyly Carte Opera Company. Members of the cast were Jeffrey Dench and Major Don Hutley and when I walked in the mess at RAF Abyad, Major Don Hutley of the Royal Corps of Signals was one of the first people I met; small world even in 1953.

The Abyad Dramatic Society was a very happy society. All ranks could be members, some acting, some behind the scenes, making the scenery or just helping in every way they could. One member was Sean Lynch who had appeared in a play with Margaret Lockwood (If he'd joined the army he might have gone to Catterick!!)

Others went on to act on TV on their return to England. The stage hands could have earned a living in the West End; perhaps they did when their National Service was over.

In 1954 we did "The Little Hut" and some very fancy effects were required by the stage manager, Alan Humphreys and his team were fantastic. After that play word came from RAF Headquarters that they would like us to put on the production for them but unfortunately all the 'effects' had been dismantled so we couldn't.

The Theatre was also used by ENSA and after the final performance celebrities were entertained by various messes in turn. The one I particularly remember was Harry Sercombe who came to the Officers' Mess.

I was standing next to an Army Colonel and an officer introduced Harry to the Colonel.

"How do you do, Colonel Galbraith?" he said.

"And this is Jean," said the officer.

"How do you do, Mrs Galbraith?" said Harry.

"I'm not married to him," I said.

"Oh you're just the Colonel's lady came the reply." He was always good for a laugh.

The Colonel was in charge of the Royal Signals contingent stationed at RAF Abyad. He was a very friendly man and well respected by his officers and men.

Sometimes during the winter months when there was little to do he would take some of us to tea at the Officer's Club. He had a car and a driver and we would sit outside and enjoy the sunshine even if it was cool.

Being associated with the Colonel made a difference when walking through the Signals to the hospital. Previously any woman walking through the camp was greeted with wolf whistles, but now when I went to visit a colleague in hospital I was greeted with, 'Evening, Ma'am!' I think I preferred the wolf whistles.

The first term passed quickly and life had settled into an easy enjoyable routine. School began at 7.40. Each morning started with our bearer Osman bringing a cup of tea and after showering we went to the Mess for breakfast. Most of the officers had already eaten and were at work very early. It was no hardship getting up as every morning was sunny and the temperature was like a glorious English summer's day.

One morning walking to the Mess I met a new arrival (you could tell he was new as he was so white and hadn't 'got his knees brown.') He smiled and said "What a glorious day."

I gave a suitable answer and thought (what's he talking about, every day is glorious).

School ended at 1.40 and we piled on the school bus with the children which meandered throughout the Fayid hirings (accommodation for service families) dropping off the children at their homes and eventually made its way to the Fayid Officers Cub where we got off. We changed into swimsuits and settled outside to have a drink and food before going out to the barge to sunbath and swim.

From the barge we could dive into the cooler clean water without the effort of wading through the hot dirty water near the shore. The barge was quite big and many people sunbathed on it away from the families and children who stayed in the shallow water. At about 4 p.m. we caught the bus back to camp, had tea did our school work and had a rest before showering and dolling up to go to the Mess for drinks and dinner.

After dinner, when it was cooler we had a variety of options. We could sit on the lawns and watch the hundreds of stars, or go into the camp Officers' Club for a drink; play darts, or put on the record player and dance.

There weren't many records but two Sid Phillips and 'Who's Sorry Now' and another record which I had never before or heard since but which I loved was, 'Why fight the feeling.'

Life was better than a holiday because it had cost me nothing and I was getting paid Burham Scale and an overseas allowance.

But as the term drew to an end we made plans for the Summer Holiday. Should I go home to the UK or go with the girls to Cyprus? We could fly home for £51 but I had only been out for three months so I opted to go to Cyprus with three friends.

This was 1953 so Cyprus was just one beautiful island. I think I had heard about Greek Cypriots or Turkish Cypriots but when we landed at Nicosia Airport they were all just Cypriots and the ones we met during our holiday were all just Cypriots and the ones we met were friendly and helpful. We stayed the night in Nicosia then the next day the four of us hired a car (I had been given driving lessons for my 21st by an uncle who was a driving instructor and it was the best present I could have received.)

I was the only one to drive and we hired a Morris Minor from Louis Touring Agency. My driving licence was used to get a licence in Cyprus so we piled our cases in the car and set off for Kyrenia where we had reserved places at the Coeur de Lia Hotel.

My companions were Maggie who was at Abyad with me, Joan who travelled out with me but was posted to Kabrit. She later cut short her contract to return to the UK. If you broke your contract within a year you paid your fare out and back but after a year you only paid the return journey. The other girl was a teacher from Deversoir. We all shared the same room and we settled in to exploring Cyprus and enjoying ourselves.

The staff were lovely, the food different but good and the weather slightly cooler than Egypt.

We had been told about the attractions in Kyrenia so couldn't wait to start our holiday.

The next morning I woke to hear Maggie chuckling. The beds were in line and she had the one near the window and I the one next to it. The sun had come pouring in at the window and falling on her bare feet which had started to burn her and woken her up. She watched as it gradually reached my feet and woke me.

We breakfasted and went out to the car and I opened it got in and got out again very quickly. The leather was red hot and I couldn't touch the steering wheel. We learned to cover the seats and wheel with towels when we left it at night.

Now there was a five mile beach and six mile beach so called because they were that distance from Kyrenia, one to the west and the other to the east.

We went to the five mile beach. It was deserted. It was a little bay with lovely sand and a little island just off the coast shore which was easy to swim to. The water was so clear and cool and it was lovely to swim, sunbathe, and when it got too hot to swim again we decided it was time to go but we had heard of this place nearby which we just had to visit. It was Mrs Newman's Farm. The story I heard was that this lady and her son had settled in Cyprus and had a farm with pedigree Jersey cows.

We ordered a pint of milk and boiled eggs. Milk! We only had the dried variety in Egypt 'this was the real stuff – white and creamy, and the eggs! Egyptian eggs were very small but there were proper eggs with yellow yolks.

After such a tea we really couldn't enjoy our dinner but we managed and then prepared to go out for the evening. We knew about the Harbour Club so that's where we went. It was owned by Judy Shirley of Monday Night at 8 o'clock fame. She had married a former Army Officer and they had set up the Club with a pianist Bill Williams. He played, she sang and it was lovely to hear them. It was such a small place that after a couple of nights there we were on first name terms. I played the piano a little, but only with music, but I did know two songs by heart. One was 'Smoke gets in Your Eyes'. I played it and she thought the introduction was superb and so said she'd sing with me playing. I'd love to say it was a success but it wasn't.

There's an art to accompanying a singer and I didn't have it. She told me to just play and ignore her but I couldn't. Still it was fun.

When it got late into the night and there was only a hard core of revellers, Bill would sing his special songs. Nowadays they wouldn't cause a lifted eyebrow, but then they were quite risqué. He sang 'The Babe that I carry' to the tune of 'The girl that I marry.'

'I'm a virgin but I'm on the verge,' 'He's got the cutest balalaika in the Balkans,' and 'The night that Spitilcosli split his tights.' A visit to the Harbour Club always rounded off the evening perfectly.

Near Kyrenia is St Hilarian Castle. It's one of the many castles Walt Disney is supposed to have used to base his castle for Snow White. Before we went I was told the road there was winding and dangerous so I was dubious about driving but it proved to be fine and we loved the castle. We also went to Bellapais Abbey where I saw a tree with both oranges and lemons on which really impressed me.

But Kyrenia was very hot in August and Maggie wanted to go somewhere cool so we decided we'd go to Troodos. Once again I had been told the road was treacherous with such hairpin bends that one had to reverse several times to get round them, and of course there were shear drops if you made a mistake. I said I'd take them to Nicosia and then they could get a bus to Troodos and I would return to Kyrenia. The night before we left I thought other people drove cars there and I was a qualified competent driver. I'd take them!

It was a lovely drive and nowhere did I have to reverse to get round bends. It was a bit like Switzerland and provided you were careful it was easy. We stopped along the route to have refreshments and the hospitality was fantastic. With a drink we were given many side dishes of delicious food before continuing our journey to Troodos.

We stayed at the Forest Park Hotel at Platres. It was so pleasant the weather cool and log fires could be lit if it turned cold. It didn't and we had a few days relaxing until we felt the need to get a little warmer and swim in the clear Mediterranean Sea so we packed our bags and returned to Kyrenia.

Near Kyrenia was Bellapais Abbey. Entrance fee was 1 shilling in 1953, and I remember it mostly because of the tree which grew under the main door and had both oranges and lemons growing on it.

Some of our gang from Abyad came on leave and we visited the Nicosia nightclubs but preferred the Harbour Club at Kyrenia. One night after it closed we drove to the five mile beach and swam out to the little island. The water was cool and refreshing and when we reached the island everything was so quiet and peaceful. As we walked up the path to the car we approached a small hotel and could hear a most peculiar noise. As we passed it we heard it was snoring in various tones from soft to raucous and there were bodies lying on the floor of the veranda and on billiard tables. We crept past, and as we drove by Mrs Newman's farm dawn was breaking and the cows were getting ready for milking.

We returned to Egypt and school started in September.

Soon it was time to start preparing for Christmas with Christmas carols and songs. By November the weather was cooler and we didn't feel the urge to spend so much time in the water. In any case we started winter hours and worked two hours in the afternoon and it was awful and I hated going back to school after lunch. We had to work the same hours as teachers in the UK so in summer we started very early but only worked mornings but in the winter we had mornings and afternoons.

Christmas in the camps started about mid-November with parties in the camp and in other stations. There was a huge raffle as usual and on 17th December the draw was held in the Mess. I won a turkey from Nairobi which was no good to me as we had no cooking facilities, but the married officers bought me a drink in exchange for the bird!

I was also the winner of a much coveted prize, a set of six pot tankards. Although they were a set the handles were all different. The first handle was a lady in a green strapless evening dress; on the second the dress had slipped. By the sixth the dress had gone and the handle was her two legs sticking out of the top of the tankard.

Quite a few people offered to buy them but I wanted to keep them as they made me laugh.

So Christmas Day came and a visit to church, then drinks in various places before Christmas dinner in the mess. The usual money was deducted from pay and then everything was free.

We started with shrimp cocktail followed by tomato soup and then roast turkey and bread sauce with chestnut stuffing or roast pork with chipolata sausage and roast potatoes, Cauliflower Mornay, French beans and garden peas.

After it was eaten and cleared away the lights were switched off and the bearers came in with flaming Christmas pudding and they marched round the room to cheering and clapping. It was eventually served with brandy sauce and this was followed by Canapés Lucile, cheese and biscuits, coffee and fruit and nuts.

Then some of the families who had had their own Christmas dinner in their quarters joined us for the dancing. My first Christmas in Egypt and it was lovely.

A week later and it was New Year's Eve. I was looking forward to this because all previous New Year's had been spent in my home. My parents were from the North East and believed in *first footing*. All the family had to be at home, father went out at five minutes to midnight and returned after the hour had been struck by the Market clock. He returned with coal and wood which was then burnt on the fire.

He was always our 'first foot' and fitted the requirements of being dark haired.

Even when I returned home from college and was over 21 I had to be in the home for the event, later I was allowed to go to the King's Head on a New Year's Eve Dance, but had to return home at 11.45 so I, too, could be at home for midnight and the New Year.

But now I am away from home and couldn't return for the occasion, I couldn't wait!

Dinner was as usual in the mess but the Ball (dance) was held in the Officers' Club on the camp. The men wore Men's Kit because we were in a hot country; the ladies were resplendent in evening gowns. As midnight approached we heard the sounds of bagpipes and two pipers in full Scottish dress came up the path and entered the building. As twelve struck the pipers played 'Auld Lang Syne' and we sang as we joined hands in a circle round them.

After that we kissed the nearest to us and I found myself and escort wedged against the piano. After a passionate embrace I looked passed him and saw a queue had formed. Most of the men had families at home in the UK so I suppose it was a good excuse for a harmless kiss at that time of year. The dance continued until the early hours when we left, some to party and others to fall into bed to sleep off the effects of the evening.

After Christmas and New Year celebrations things were a little quieter on the social front. The weather was cool so swimming for most of us was out of the question; so it was cinema, concerts from ENSA, darts, dinner at the Officers' Club, or the Greek Club at Fanara.

The colonel in command of the Royal Signals on the camp organised Scottish Dancing in the Abyad Officers Club an activity which was only suitable for the winter. A crowd of us who had been enjoying a few drinks in the Mess sauntered over and watched. I had once been a member of the St. Aidens Scottish Dancing Society at Catterick Camp and kept asking for strip the 'widow' (willow) a fast dance where couples, when they are at the top of the set spin down the line twisting and twirling each person in the line and their partner.

I suppose the colonel got fed up with the barracking and eventually played the record and my partner and I joined in the dance. All went well until I reached the colonel who spun me and let go very suddenly, I was flung against the wall and sobered up very quickly. The colonel was most apologetic but I never visited his dances again.

We learned a few words in Arabic; just enough to get by, after all the only Egyptians we met were the bearers, the waiters in the Mess and shop keepers in Fayid. They all spoke enough English for us to understand each other. Our bearer, Osman, had been bearer to other airmen before he came to us so his vocabulary included a few words not usually used in polite society.

One morning as we were preparing to go to work I heard Olwen in her plummy posh voice ask where I was as we were going to walk to school together. I heard Osman reply Mem Sahib in the shit house. He couldn't understand why Olwen and the others smiled and turned away.

We eventually got another bearer, Abdullah, and he was a lovely man. He was only small but very friendly and polite and a hard worker, not that there was much to do with half a dozen women but he was always so willing and helpful. He had just had a daughter, Leila, and was so proud of her so I asked if he could bring her to see us which he did. She was only about four months old and a bonny girl whom he obviously adored and he was so proud to show her to us.

Another time they had a celebration in Fayid village. We always knew when they were partying as we could hear the noise in the village just over the road from the camp.

I asked Osman what they did and he said they danced.

"With women?"

"No," he replied, and laughed at such a suggestion, "with sticks."

"Sticks" I said, "what do you do with them?"

He gave a giggle and said they waved them over their heads. Judging by the noise they made it must have been an energetic enjoyable dance.

Another time Abdullah brought me a present from some celebration. It was a sugar confectionary which I suppose was edible. It was in the shape of a man on a horse and he was carrying the Egyptian flag and it was about ten inches high and much too good to break up and eat, so I kept it as an ornament.

I wonder what happened to all the people who worked on camp after we left.

The Officers' Club in Fayid advertised an evening of entertainment which included dinner and dancing and a belly dancer. As things were fairly quiet during the first four months of the year we decided to go. The belly dancer was the real thing and so unlike the Hollywood versions. It was the first we had seen and everything but everything quivered. It was perpetual motion and we were fascinated and the conversation in the Staff Room next day centred on the dancer and in the midst of this conversation Mr Strong walked in.

As I have said he had worked in Cairo prior to teaching with the RAF. At the silence on his entry he looked a bit nonplussed so I said "We were discussing the belly dancer at the Officers' Club last night. She was very good indeed."

He cleared his throat as was his want and said "Ah yes, the first belly dancer I saw was in a brothel in Cairo."

There was a stunned silence, I mean what can one say after that, remember this was 1954 and 'brothel' was not a word one associated with a headmaster.

We went to the cinema quite a lot. Often, Jack, a great cinema goer would see us in the bar at lunch time and as he bought a ticket would ask if we wanted to go with him and if nothing else was happening we went. Outside the cinema would be an Egyptian selling peanuts and Maggie would say "I'll buy you a packet because you are not having any of mine."

I liked to decline the offer and then eat some of hers during the picture. And of course I enjoyed my amateur dramatics that were put on during the winter months. We put on a production of 'Mountain Air' in which in one scene I had to wear a swimsuit. By this time all the swimsuits I had brought with me had had a good deal of wear and were a little too tatty to be worn on stage, so I got someone who was going to Cyprus to bring me one back. It was rather nice, red with a panel of white stripes down the front. Unfortunately it was a little snug but it would be alright. On the first night the CO of the station was on the front row.

After the performance I got the message "Change the costume," I didn't, after all I had bought it specially for the show and it wasn't as bad as all that. I didn't hear anything else, the audience seemed to like the play and that's the main thing.

The Education Officers decided to put on a conference – Cyprus at Easter. They 'asked' Maggie, and myself to attend and give a five minute talk on any subject to do with education. We decided we would rather go on holiday to Cyprus and we were informed no teacher would be allowed to go for the Easter so we decided the only way we would get there was to go to their conference. She decided to talk on Libraries in Schools. I racked my brains, and came up with 'Drama in Schools.' Five minutes isn't long when you are enjoying yourself but speaking in front of twenty RAF officers it was an eternity. But we got to Cyprus for Easter and the two Tommies (our two squadron leaders) got leave and came as well.

Cyprus was so cold, Egypt was bad but Cyprus was no better. Obviously swimming was out but there was Nicosia where the conference was held and we hired a car and went to our haunts in the North of the island, Kyrenia and Bellapais on the five mile beach and a trip to Mrs Newman's farm.

In the evening we went night clubbing. We had heard of one place but when we got there as we went down the stairs to the club was a notice 'No service Personnel allowed.'

The two Tommies wanted to go back but we ventured further. There was sawdust on the floor and a sign which said 'Don't spit on the floor.' We decided it wasn't the place for us and we all went on to the Femina night club. Maggie and her Tommy went to the bar and the other Tommy and I sat by the dance floor where there was a cabaret being performed. He sat behind me and I leaned against him, as we sat drinking and watching, a waiter came to Tommy and handed him a note. He opened it and showed it to me. It said 'The way that you sit is not proper and will you please respect the Management."

We looked at each other, and then laughed thinking that Maggie and Tommy had sent it. We went and joined them at the bar to tell them what we thought about it but they assured us they had not sent it. It really was from The Management so we decided to leave and went on to the Chantclare.

Easter Monday came, and it was a different world, the sun was shining, it was hot and summer had arrived. We thoroughly enjoyed our weekend and went back to Abyad refreshed and ready for the summer term.

We decided to join the Phoenix Sailing Club, not that we were keen on sailing but it would be a change from the

Officers' Club. There were quite a few yachts owned by the Club and plenty of instructors to teach people new to sail them. They were qualified to test people and award certificates. I wasn't interested in sailing although I had once spent a holiday in Holland sailing with friends on the canals so I knew what to do and would crew for anyone if they needed anyone. Some of the men from the Mess bought a barge and I bought a canoe.

The fellows helped me to paint it and I got letters from school and stencilled its name ROBIN on the side. A friend from stores got me some 'biscuits' to put in the bottom of it and it was lovely. The water on the edge of the lake was warm and muddy but just a little way and it was cool and clear.

After school, I would get the school bus to the lake, have lunch have a little paddle in my canoe and drop over the side for a swim and after a drink and gossip return in time to shower, do school work, and then go to dinner in the Mess.

At 4 o'clock the wind would rise on the Bitter Lake and you could almost set your watch by it. One day I lingered a little longer than usual and at 4 o'clock the wind came up and I was quite a way out and couldn't get back.

Fortunately a yacht was coming in and they gave me a tow. Then I helped with their chores. I think that's what put me off sailing, having to wash the boat and sails etc. before leaving.

Every so often they held Regattas up and down the Bitter Lake. One Regatta was at Fanara and the Phoenix Club was getting organised to attend. The Commodore of the Phoenix was a group captain from Abyad and he was very nice. He was very approachable and good company but it was understandable that other ranks and junior officers didn't particularly want to crew for him. I didn't either but he was the commander and he should be there so he persuaded me to go with him.

Of course we had to sail down to Fanara and at first we made good time and then the boat drifted, wind dropped completely and the sails slumped.

I sunbathed whilst he ranted and raved that we weren't going to be there for the first race. Eventually the wind picked up and we made it in time but everyone came up to me at odd moments chuckling away and asking me how I'd got on, on the journey down when the wind had dropped. There were many nudges and winks but he had been perfectly proper and on the whole good company. But I didn't do it again.

One of the teachers, Sally, who came out on the same plane had then posted to Kabrit at the southern end of the Bitter Lake. It was a quiet station and far from shops and clubs. Their quarters were near the lake so very handy for a swim. Unfortunately the lake at that part was an ideal habitat for leeches. When I went there for the Coronation Ball, I had a very enjoyable time apart from coming out of the water screaming because of all the leeches which had to be picked off individually. I wouldn't have liked that posting and neither did Sally. She stayed for a year and then paid for her own flight home.

If she hadn't stayed for one year she would have had to pay for her flight out as well as back.

Deversoir was a fighter station north of Fayid and further north was the town of Ishmalia. I went there twice, once with a man from my home town who was finishing his National Service tour and one with an officer who had a meeting then and asked me if I would like to accompany him to see the place.

He went off to his meeting and we arranged to meet later in the afternoon. The shops closed at midday and I wandered around and it was so hot. I was exhausted when we met up and on my return; listening to the radio it said the temperature in Ishmalia had been 109 degrees in the shade. That's hot!

Liz came out and the first night she came to my room as I said I would take her to the Mess for dinner and show her the ropes. She was wearing a cotton dress with a cardigan. I stared at her and asked why she was wearing a woolly and she replied "Listen to that wind it must be cold outside." I explained it was the Hamsin, a wind which blew for days on end and caused sand storms, but it was hot. When we opened the door to go outside the hot blast was like opening an oven door.

I introduced her to our 'gang' so she wouldn't feel so alone. They were like-minded fellows who made the best of things and were waiting for the time when their wives and families could join them either in a hiring of forces quarters on the camp. One of the Royal Signals officers, who would eat the rim of his glass when he had had a few and was in a party mood, had been a paratrooper. Another RAF officer had been one of The Dam Busters and one night he and the paratrooper got together. One sat on a stool, the other stood on a bar stool behind him.

They pretended they were doing a drop over enemy lines and after they had dodged the flak the time came for the drop and the para jumped and rolled over on the floor. How he avoided breaking his neck or even the odd bone I don't know. The para believed all pain was relative and he would thump his fist into the wall and say he didn't feel a thing. I'm glad he was on our side.

When the wives came out the men moved out of the mess, but we still continued to go to their parties at their homes and of course taught the children.

One of the officers, a wing commander, was moved to Fanara and he and his wife were given a boat as their quarters. They invited me to Fanara to stay on the boat for a weekend and it was lovely. The boat didn't move, of course, it had been moved up to a quarry where the engine had been taken out and the space made into a lounge. At one end they had their quarters and bedroom and bathroom and at the other end were the quarters for a guest which again had its own bathroom.

It was lovely to sit on the deck in the evening enjoying a last drink of the day under the stars.

RAF Abyad was like a little town situated between RAF Fayid and Fayid Town. Opposite was Fayid village where most of the bearers and civilian workers lived. The camp contained living quarters for married and single personnel, churches, Post office run by the Arms Postal Service, a NAAFI, a hospital and of course all the different messes. It covered quite a large area and was surrounded by barbed wire and patrolled constantly.

Occasionally they would make an extra effort for security and once crossing from the Teachers quarters to the Mess for dinner I was stopped by a fully armed guard with the well-known shout of "Who Goes There?" To say I was startled is an understatement, it was dark I was alone and a man pointing a gun at me, a perfectly innocent civilian. I stammered "Well it's me." It wasn't the reply he was expecting but he lowered his rifle and allowed me to pass.

The Egyptians we met, in shops and in camp were very civil and friendly, but we did hear stories about some unpleasant encounters. We were told some had been 'flashing' at some married women from RAF Fayid. The women were told to say an Arabic phrase if it happened again. It did and they repeated their Arabic at which the offender hastily dropped his galabeya and shuffled away. The phrase translated said "Is that all?" I don't know if it's true but it's a good story.

One of the Officers in the Mess was having a birthday at the Officers Club in Fayid and had invited many people from Abyad. Maggie had been invited with her boyfriend, some nurses with boyfriends and me but not my boyfriend. I asked Maggie if he was hoping I would be his partner for the evening and she said, "Ask him." I did

Not so bluntly, but I worked the conversation round as to why my partner had not been invited and he said he had invited many army officers who hadn't partners and he had said he would get some they could dance with. I thought I might meet someone I had known at Catterick after all the first day I walked into the Abyad Mess I met Major Don Hutley who had been in the Cary Theatre Club and had produced one of their plays.

I had also met a girl I had been to school with who was married to an army officer. I went to her hiring for dinner and broke a glass as I was drying the dishes. She was very upset as she had to pay for breakages so I wasn't invited back. So I thought it would be a change to meet lots of new people so I went.

I sat at the top table and it was quite obvious I was birthday boy's partner as I didn't particularly like him and I felt I had been tricked; I was livid. After dinner I went to Maggie and said I was going back to camp. She said to wait a little longer and she and Tommy would come, too, but she was obviously enjoying herself so I told her to stay and I would go.

I caught a taxi outside and the driver took me to the camp gate (they weren't allowed in) and as I got out he said "Memsahib, you should not travel alone, there are many dangers. If you must do it make sure it is my taxi you use."

I realised I had been stupid and thanked him. Not an enjoyable evening but I went to the camp Officers' Mess and had a drink with people I liked.

The summer holidays came around again and many of the teachers decided to leave Egypt for other exotic places. The RAF would take you anywhere if they had a seat available but if they couldn't bring you back you had to pay your own fare on a schedule flight and depending on where you went that could be very expensive. So most of them opted for Cyprus, Jordan and Turkey but Maggie and I decided to return to UK and visit our parents and friends.

The flight cost about £50 return and they guaranteed a seat on a return flight in time for the new school year.

Weeks before the holiday we spent every afternoon on the beach getting what was commonly known as a 'Panic Tan.' The day before we left we were Guinea Gold (nearly all over). I went to pay my Mess bill and the officer looked at me and asked when I was leaving. When I told him it was the next day he said "I hope you peel!"

So on July 15th, St. Swithin's Day we flew to Stansted and it was pouring. It rained, and rained for the next 40 days and my Guinea Gold changed to mellow yellow and dirty white. But the first few days and with family and friends was lovely. My mother delighted in lifting the hem of my skirt and showing everyone my brown legs but as the colour faded that soon stopped.

But it was lovely to see all the shops with lovely clothes. In Egypt we had the NAAFI which had limited stock. If you went there when it was put on display there was little to buy. There were a few local 'tailors' in Fayid and they weren't bad although they hadn't much choice of materials. I had one evening dress made of white 'sharkskin.'

It was strapless and had a long flared skirt. It looked elegant, especially with a tan and when I danced it swirled around my legs. Unfortunately at a dance in Fanara doing a tango with a very good partner, as he swung me over his knee, he trod on the hem and the strapless became topless!

I showed where the tan ended! There was a lovely shop Eva in Ledra Street in Nicosia and every time I went to Cyprus I called in at the shop asked to see all the dresses in my size and bought quite a few.

Even so it was lovely to visit shops in Newcastle and Darlington and get new clothes for the rest of my tour in Egypt. And then on the news came the bombshell. The Egyptians had abrogated the Treaty and we were all going to leave. I wondered if I would get a cable to say "As you're in UK stay there." Fortunately it didn't arrive and we were taken back to finish our tour.

Maggie and I arrived back to camp and walked into the Mess. All our friends jeered and said we looked like "Moon men," the name given to new comers who weren't tanned. In the next few days we were on the beach, sun-oiled, burning, and suffering to get that gorgeous tan again.

Air Ministry contacted us to see where we would like to go. Maggie opted for Jordan, I wanted Habbaniyah, others went to Cyprus and Singapore. Everyone got their wish except me; they were sending the children home from Habbaniyah, so I said I'd go where they needed someone. But that was a while yet it would take quite a time to pack up and move.

So Christmas came with all the celebrations. Perhaps as it was to be the last the British Forces spent in Egypt it was more festive and energetic than usual but by February I was looking forward to my next holiday in Cyprus. One of our newer teachers hadn't been before so I said I would take her round the island as I felt I knew it quite well by now. She was only staying for a few days so we had a lot to pack into the holiday.

On arriving in Nicosia the first thing we did was hire a car and as usual I got one from the Louis Touring Agency. They had always given good service even when, I had had a puncture in the 'pan handle', (the north west of the island.)

Once we were mobile we set about finding accommodation. I parked outside a hotel and Milly went inside to see if they had vacancies. As I sat there a man standing on the veranda asked if the hire car was satisfactory. I wondered how he knew it was hired as it had no markings on it.

"I'm Mr Louis" he replied to my question. I told him as always I was very pleased with his cars.

Just as we settled into our room a waiter knocked on the door and asked us if we would join Mr Louis for a drink but as we made other arrangements we had to decline his offer.

Next morning we were up bright and early to make a tour of the island but first we had arranged with Liz who was on holiday in the hotel with her boyfriend to drop her in Nicosia. I pulled into a line of stationary cars to drop her and on turning my head to pull out of the line; I twisted my neck and was in agony. Our journey to Limassol was awful; I couldn't turn my head to the left so every time we came to a junction I had to ask Milly if the way was clear. Fortunately there was little traffic around the main town in Cyprus in those days so the journey was uneventful.

We wandered round Limassol and then set off to Paphos. I lost my way a bit as there were so many one way streets and I kept finding myself in the town again but eventually by the castle we found the right route and set off for Paphos where we planned to stay the night. We found a lovely hotel.

There weren't many in those days. The weather was gorgeous, not too hot the food was good but my neck was still very painful. I asked the hotel if there was a doctor I could see and they sent us to the hospital. A really nice doctor examined my neck. He spoke no English but a nurse translated for us. He said there was nothing seriously wrong, it would be alright within a few days and he gave me some pain killers. When I asked what I owed him he smiled and the nurse said "The cost is nothing but if you want to put something in the charity box we would be grateful."

I did and by the next morning my neck was a little easier.

Again, an early start to make our way to Kyrenia, there wasn't much in the way of habitation but the road was good the views beautiful and we were enjoying the drive.

Milly is one of those people who cannot go long without food and before long she was looking for some place to buy something. Travelling through a little town called Morphou she spotted a tavern cum shop with bread and fruit in the window and she asked me to stop which I did. I switched off the engine and enjoyed my surroundings when the door opened, a white-faced Milly clutching her provisions shouted at me to drive on quickly. It was such a peaceful place I asked whatever was the matter.

"Drive on drive on I'll tell you later."

There was no one else about and I couldn't see why she was so upset.

“Drive on,” she screamed so I started the car and drove out of the town quickly. When we were clear of the town I slowed down and asked her for an explanation.

She had walked into the taverna where a few men were sitting at the tables. She asked for some bread and bananas and took out her purse to pay. All the men got up and surrounded her. They didn’t say a word and she was terrified. She snatched the food and ran to the car and it took her some time to calm down. On our return to Egypt we read in a newspaper that there had been a riot in the College at Morphou so I suppose she had every right to be frightened.

We arrived in Kyrenia and booked in at the Bristol Hotel. Here everything was calm and serene and we set out to show her the area. I love Kyrenia; the five mile beach, the six mile beach, St. Hilarian Castle. Bellapais Abbey and of course Mrs Newman’s Farm where we stopped for a pint of milk and boiled egg. She loved the area and enjoyed going round the places again and we ended our evening at the Harbour Club.

Apart from the hiccup at Morphou the holiday had been restful and most enjoyable and the next morning we returned to Nicosia. Milly went back to Egypt and I thought I’d stay a couple of days longer and just relax.

Liz and her boyfriend had other ideas. When they heard I planned to stay in the hotel to have a meal they insisted that I go with them for a meal and then have one drink in the Femina and then they would put me in a taxi to return to the hotel. We had a lovely meal and arrived at the Femina early before the place had warmed up. A pianist was at the grand piano and a few people were on bar stools round the piano listening to him play.

I noticed a man at the other side of the piano and he kept looking at me. I have a good memory for faces and I recognised him but he obviously couldn’t place me. Eventually he wandered round and said “I know it sounds corny but haven’t we met before?”

I said “Well if you’re Ian Campbell well yes we have met.”

“I knew it,” he said was it in Hong Kong?”

“No.”

“South Africa?”

“No.”

He went round the world before he gave up and said “Well where was it?”

“Catterick Camp.”

He was in the Royal Signals and we were members of the same society but had never actually talked to each other. He was stationed in Egypt and had organised football matches between Canal Zone series and Cyprus Service personnel. He was enjoying an evening with his team and he insisted that I accompany them to a Greek nightclub. So much for my quiet night! Unfortunately the Greek nightclub was closed as it was a holiday but they let us in and put on a show for us.

Well it was all Greek to me but even though I couldn’t understand it I had to laugh when a man dressed as a baby was pushed around in a pram.

The team picked me up in the morning to go shopping and then I returned to Egypt in the afternoon.

That evening having dinner with my current escort, a doctor, I was telling him about my holiday especially about my neck which was still quite painful. He got up; stood behind me with his hands each side of my head he yanked it. I thought he’d broken my neck I’m sure he knew what he was doing but it did hurt and I don’t think his action did anything to help.

He was a gynaecologist and of course competence in that department was needed on a large camp with wives and female personnel, teachers, WVS, WAAFS, NAAFI.

These were the doctors and specialists but most complaints were to do with “Gyppy Tummy” which must have affected everyone at some time or another.

The remedy was 'Kaolin and Morph' a white emulsion which wasn't unpleasant to the taste and cleared up the infection very quickly. However dysentery was a different matter. I managed to get it in 1956 after a cocktail party at Deversoir.

It was held in the open air and there were a few flies buzzing around so I suppose it could be expected. Anyway I was put into hospital in a very nice room and given pills. There were very many of them in fact I seem to remember there were 500 to be taken in five days at 100 a day in batches of 20, perhaps time has exaggerated the number but there were an awful lot. I had to drink a full bottle of squash a day diluted of course to prevent the formation of kidney stones. It was not very pleasant but once I had started the treatment I began to improve. The WVS who did a marvellous job in Abyad came round with 'goods,' I bought a tablecloth to embroider. It helped to pass the time. I called it my 'dysentery cloth,' which was a bit off-putting to visitors having a cup of tea and sandwich in later times.

I had one other session in hospital for the removal of my wisdom teeth. A wing commander from RAF Fayid came to do the operation but I never met him. He arrived after I had been anaesthetised and left before my recovery and I never saw him at all. Later in Amman the dentist giving me a check-up said "I see you have had your wisdom teeth removed."

It appears he needed his doing but wouldn't have the operation because he knew how it was performed and didn't relish the idea. I knew nothing of the procedure so I awoke to find a nurse and Maggie waiting for me to regain consciousness. I was immediately sick with copious quantities of blood, and remained in hospital for a few days. I had the operation at half term so that I wouldn't miss work. My mouth had split at each corner and my cheeks were chubby and rosy. The stitches had a few loose ends but when they had been removed and my cuts had healed and my cheeks resumed their normal shape and colour I was as good as new.

I hadn't had any trouble with wisdom teeth but my dentist could see it coming so gave me the choice of having them out before they caused trouble or waiting until they did so I opted for the former. The worst part of the whole operation was the penicillin jabs I was given in my bottom. I learned to dread the nurse coming in with that little dish containing a syringe. It hurt much worse than the operation itself.

The room I was given in the hospital was next to the nurse's staff room. It was so noisy and I was woken during the night with laughter and talking. I asked them to be quiet which they were for a while and then gradually it would start again. It seemed so silly putting a staff room next to recovery room when there were other rooms which could have been used.

I was never actually told that men were not allowed into women's quarters but it was understood that it was a court martial offence for the man if he was found there. Perhaps the men had been told that but when we mentioned it we always had a laugh and joke about it.

One night a man ran down the veranda at the back of our rooms. He screamed and shouted but it was all over in a minute we didn't hear what he said and by the time we were out of bed he had gone. I think he was probably dared by others and although we reported it nothing came of the incident.

Usually we said goodnight to our escorts at the gap in the sacking which served as an entrance to our quarters. It was illuminated by a security light which we named 'The Star of Bethlehem' but sometimes especially during the day or at holiday times men came into our area and had tea or drinks with us.

We never seriously thought that anyone would be court martialled. But one Sunday lunch time after a few drinks in the club, Olwen and a squadron leader were obviously getting on very well. As we left I said "You don't mind getting court martialled then?" and he was off like a frightened rabbit. She turned on me and told me in no uncertain terms it was nothing to do with me and to mind my own business.

We had a big party in my room to celebrate my birthday. We had about thirty people there and there was music and singing and as they couldn't all fit in my room they spilled over into the sand outside. I don't know whether someone had asked permission but it was certainly no secret and nothing was said.

However one Saturday night my doctor friend escorted me to The Star and I was teasing him and we were making quite a noise, he picked me up and carried me to my room, threw me on the bed and left.

Monday at the end of school Mr Strong asked all the staff to come to the staff room where a Squadron Leader Mitler was waiting to speak to us all. It had been reported to him by one of the WAAF Sergeants that a man had entered our room "last night." He asked us all if that was so and everyone said, "No." so he asked us all individually and everyone again said, "No." I am a very poor liar but I said no because no one had been to my room on the Sunday night. As he left he said "Or another night?" so everyone, except me said no.

As I walked with Liz across the sand to our rooms I told Liz about my friend and how I felt a bit guilty, but she calmed me down and said it was stupid anyway and no one took any notice of it.

When I told my friend he was furious. He said he knew who had reported it, I won't say what he said about her but he finished, "If she ever comes to see me professionally she'll suffer." As he was the gynaecologist I hated to think what he could do but as he started to laugh I knew he was joking.

So Abyad began to close down. Maggie had gone off to Amman at Easter as our numbers dwindled, Liz was going to Cyprus and I was asked to go to Amman in August ready for the September term.

A big party was arranged the night before I left. I had made many friends and they wanted me to remember my last night in Egypt. Two days before the parting I felt ill, by the afternoon of the party I knew I had dysentery again. The doctor gave me the pills all 500 of them and told me to report to the doctor as soon as I reached Amman. So I missed my party. I managed to get to the plane but I felt awful. It stopped me remembering all the friends I was leaving whether I would ever see them again.

The Central Forces Radio broadcast many UK shows, Educating Archie and Stanley Holloway show etc. but it also ran broadcasts of its own.

The Station was manned by Forces personnel and I suppose they worked in their free time. Maggie happened to meet one of the organisers and he asked her if she would appear in twenty questions as the guest. They always had three residents and one guest. They wanted a school teacher as their guest but she declined but said she knew someone who would do me! After some hesitation I agreed and duly turned up at the station to make the recording. The three residents were good; after all they had been doing it for a while. I felt out of my depth at first but the member of the panel who was excellent pulled out of his pocket a nail file and began to clean his nails.

Light dawned; "A nail file" I shouted and it was correct, of course the actress didn't know I had been helped but later in the programme I did answer "A sausage" all on my own efforts.

I was asked to return not in twenty questions but to do an excerpt of a play in which I was Clytemnestra and I remember I had to scream. After my first rehearsal I was asked if I couldn't scream any louder! After that I really let rip and thoroughly enjoyed myself.

We had plans to do *Fanny by Gaslight* and I was very disappointed when it fell through. Still a radio broadcast to

America when I was 16, a broadcast in the UK when amateur reps were featured, and now one in Egypt isn't bad for an assistant school ma'am.

Eighteen months in Egypt and no chance of seeing the Pyramids and Sphinx. How could anyone say they had lived in Egypt and not visited Cairo and the sights! But in December 1954 the Egyptian authorities knew that the British had agreed to leave, relented and allowed us in for a day. We piled into the buses and set off for Cairo. It was wonderful. The Sphinx with his damaged nose, the pyramids, and the camels all appeared like a living travel book. Of course it was winter so we were wearing warm coats but that was preferable to sightseeing in blazing hot sunshine.

We visited the Mohammed Ali Mosque so much different from our own churches. We removed our shoes and put on the slippers which were provided. Inside the building was a huge space beautifully carpeted but with no seats. High up on a wall was the pulpit from which the preacher could see all the worshippers in the floor below.

Then on we went to the Cairo Museum. I wish I had known more about the splendours I was about to see and realised what a privilege it was to see the Tutankhamen treasures. But before we saw them we saw all the 'coffins' which seemed to be stacked at the entrance hall of the museum. They all had the 'eye' at the side and we were told that when the coffin was placed outside the city it was put so that the 'eye' could look on the living and keep a check on them.

We had to go through a turnstile to enter the Tutankhamen area and there were guards all around. Everything was behind glass I suppose to stop thieving and also to keep them in good condition. I could have stayed longer but as we only had one day in Cairo we moved on to the south to barter and buy mementos.

Everyone was so pleasant and seemed pleased to see us and why not? Tourists provide money and Egypt had such a lot to offer in the way to sightseers.

It was a marvellous day and as we arrived back at Abyad I was satisfied that I had seen some of the magnificent sights of Cairo although I didn't realise at the time how fortunate I was to see Tutankhamen treasure in Cairo.

So next stop Amman, the capital of Jordan. The RAF plane landed at Mafraq and we walked across to the hut through six inches of dust. It was just like talcum powder and each footstep threw up clouds of the dust. I made some comment about the need for a path or something to make walking easier to a fellow passenger who obviously knew the area, he said in the spring this area would be a mass of beautiful wild flowers and that this 'dust' was filled with seeds. As it was August I found it hard to believe that this dust plain would be a mass of colour in a few months' time but of course it was.

Maggie had come to Amman at Easter and I suppose she expected to be housed in the Officers' Mess as we had been in Egypt. But that was not to be. There was no room in the Mess and certainly not for ladies. It was quite a small station and there were single storey buildings in the form of a square. In the centre was a concrete area which was used for dancing in summer and then there were a few flower beds round that and the accommodation beyond that. One side was the communal area of bar, lounge and dining room.

At first Maggie was housed with a family who agreed to her living with them until she found a place for us to rent. Just outside the camp, flats were being built and were due to be completed in a few weeks so she arranged with an RAF officer who spoke Arabic to meet the owner and to rent one of the flats. She paid three months' rent in advance and signed an agreement. Every so often she wandered to the site to see how things were progressing and was annoyed to see that all the flats were taking shape except for ours where work was at a standstill. She saw the man in charge and with signs let him know she was worried about the small amount of work being done on our flat and he with signs told her not to worry everything was ok.

She was especially worried when on one of her visits he told her, the three months were up and she now needed to pay the next month's rent. She contacted the officer who had negotiated the contract and he pointed out to the overseer that the three months already paid were to start from when the occupants were in the flat and therefore we would not be paying anything until we had been in the flat for three months. They argued but it was in black and white and the agreement had to be honoured.

All the workers were transferred to our flat and within a short time it was completed. Maggie rented the furniture from a place in Amman so when I arrived I was lucky enough to have accommodation. She had nicknamed the overseer Bandit Number One. When I arrived she introduced him as that, and he grinning at me said "Yes I Bandit Number One."

He knew what we meant and delighted in his name. He was a magnificent figure, tall with a black beard and national dress and he had the most beautiful dagger tucked into his belt. We saw a lot of him because they still had the rest of the flats to complete. There were four altogether and they were planning another two above us but they were never built whilst we lived there.

So I had arrived in Amman. I met Maggie at the camp and she took me to the flat which was just outside the perimeter fence. That evening we went to the Mess and in the full bar I was introduced to a few members and as I weighed them up I knew they were giving me the once over as well.

I suppose it was quite an occasion as Maggie and I were the only single females on the camp apart from daughters. We were given full membership of the Mess but the wives and daughters, if they came to the Mess had to sit in the Ladies Room whilst husbands brought their drinks. They were allowed in the rest of the Mess on high days and holidays and dance nights. The prospect was rather nice, a single female on a RAF fighter station!

The first night was not a success. I had left many friends in Abyad, in fact I should think I was the longest serving member of the Mess, having been there for nearly 2 ½ years. And now I was among strangers and fighter pilots who are a different breed from a Maintenance Unit.

Then I spotted a dart board. Now I had never played darts until I went to Abyad and we had spent many happy hours in the Officers Club playing either in our own or in pairs or teams. It helped to pass the time away and as the loser bought the drinks and I picked my partners well, by the end of the evening we were in a merry frame of mind. In fact one of my biggest disappointments was playing in a team and the winners received a silver cup.

Wez, a flight lieutenant I met on my first night in Abyad, and I were by far the best team but this particular day we could not finish on a double. We had many chances but missed them all and I didn't win a silver engraved cup!

Anyway, I spotted the dart board and thinking it would ease the atmosphere I suggested a game of darts.

DARTS, there was silence; "We don't play darts here," I was told. So my talent with the small arrow was never discovered and I don't think I've played darts since.

Having arrived late because of my 'problem' and getting the all clear from the doctor I arrived at school after the term had started. Mr Strong had taken over as head earlier in the year so I felt at home straight away. It was a small school. Miss Miller had arrived from Abyad 18 months before and she took the infants and lived in a nunnery in Amman. The other teachers were wives of RAF personnel and very friendly and pleasant. Once again Maggie had the 10 –11 year olds and I had the 8 – 9s.

As I had arrived late there was quite a bit of mail waiting for me. One day as I was checking if there were any letters a voice behind said "So you're Miss Hood, I wondered who the person was with a name so like mine."

Turning around a saw a tall man in priest's garb who introduced himself as Father Hoad. He came to the camp often to collect his mail and have a meal and a chat with people. He was a Catholic priest and I understood he was something to do with the Garden of Gethsemane and the Church of all Nations in Jerusalem. There wasn't a Catholic padre on the camp so I presume he took services. We did have a C of E padre and another denominations padre.

On Saturday night there was a dance, an opportunity to relax and meet some of the wives. So with hair washed and a long evening dress on I arrived at the dance which was held in the 'concrete square'. It always seemed such a shame that the ladies wore their glamorous long ball dresses and then danced on roads and walked on sand. The hemline very quickly became tatty and dirty which spoiled the whole effect. I wore one of my tatty hemmed ones in the play the Little Hut. As I was supposed to be shipwrecked the state of the hem didn't matter but the dress got shorter and shorter as we performed the play as the cast kept tearing off the really ragged pieces.

Anyway there I was in a fairly new ball gown at my first dance. Fortunately one of the pilots had just arrived and the two of us being new comers got on well. We didn't mix with the families but it was a pleasant evening and Will the newcomer and I agreed to meet at the swimming pool the next day.

Swimming pool? Well it was a static water tank and a far cry from the Bitter Lake swimming in Egypt. It was crowded with families and children and eventually when I saw Will we had a swim but it wasn't very pleasant and my visits were limited to taking the children for their swimming lesson.

One little girl swam half a mile and got a certificate for it. She was only about 7 and she had to be lifted out of the water at the end. I decided I'd do it to get the certificate so flayed up and down the pool until I had done the requested number of lengths.

Where's my certificate?

We've run out of them but will give you one when the new ones arrive.

They never did. No darts cup, no swimming certificate, the only thing I won was a highly commended for my painting at an Arts and Crafts Exhibition at Fayid. And that's a fraud because it was painting by numbers which my cousin had sent from America. The Major in charge had persuaded me to put it in because they had so few paintings; when I received my certificate I said "But it's painting by numbers and not original."

"Ah, he said you got it because the brush work was so good!"

He didn't add "and there were few entries!"

Just as I was settling in, the Squadron stationed in Amman were sent to Cyprus on exercises and the Squadron from Habbaniyah moved in. Once again I felt like a stranger. I went to the Mess to collect my mail and in the bar were two men of 249 Squadron, Will and Tony who had come to collect the squadron's mail to take back to Cyprus. They too felt like strangers in their own Mess so we decided to adjourn to the flat with a bottle and make our own fun. Arriving at the flat Maggie had already gone to bed so the three of us tiptoed into my bedroom so as not to disturb her. Our bedrooms were on each side of the lounge. I collected some glasses and we settled down to a few jokes and a little merriment until the lads decided it was time to go. We were all fairly merry and as Will and Tony lurched down the stairs they called out "Bring out your dead" several times in loud voices.

As the OD Padre lived in the flat below I tried to shush them but to no avail. They staggered off in the night and after closing the door I returned inside. Maggie was just coming out of the bathroom and she was very cross indeed. "I hope you don't think this is going to happen often," she said.

Now no one loved a party better than Maggie and after a few Pernods, her favourite tipple she was not the most staid character. I can only assume she was sorry she had missed the 'party', so with a parting, "Well you should have joined us," I swept into my bedroom and forgot about the incident.

Maggie's boyfriend from Egypt was coming for a few days and she organised a visit to Petra for the three of us. 'Petra the rose red city half as old as time itself', had only been re-discovered earlier in the century and had been on a trade route from Egypt to Jerusalem and was inhabited by the Nabateans. It had been hewn out of the 'red rose' rock and was only accessible through a long rift in the rocks.

We had been told the only accommodation was in a fort at Ma'am so we were told to take our own sheets. The Arab Legion agreed to take us in a small aircraft to Ma'an and they would arrange for a truck to take us outside Petra where there would be three horses to walk us into Petra itself.

We caught the plane but before it landed it had to circle to chase the sheep off the 'runway.'

On landing we were told there was a hotel nearby, where we could stay the night. We arrived at the hotel and were shown to our room. As we walked up the stairs there were framed letters on the walls expressing the visitors delight and recommendations for the hotel. Of course they were dated in the 1920s and in that time it must have been better than a tent.

Maggie and I shared a room and Tommy stayed with a regiment, the Queen's Bays at Maan. We picked our beds and mine had a pair of slippers beneath it and the sheets were filthy so we used the sheets we had bought to remake the bed.

On asking for the bathroom we were shown a huge room with a toilet at one end, raised on a pedestal. It looked like a throne and the seat was so heavily carved it was quite uncomfortable I suppose it did stop anyone lingering on in comfort.

After a meal we retired for the night, as it was warm I wanted the window open. Maggie wanted it closed as the mosquito netting was full of holes. I won and the window was opened.

The next morning I awoke ready for the day in Petra. Maggie awoke and screamed, "I look like Dracula's daughter." She did. The mosquitos had flown in and found her very tasty and across her forehead you could see where one had made his way having a little nibble at frequent intervals. Her forehead was so swollen and quite painful but I had escaped altogether. It was a good thing we were only spending one night there so we had breakfast and left leaving no letter of recommendation.

We mounted our horses to complete the entry to Petra. Fortunately they were led by little Arab boys as neither of us had ridden before. It was an hour's journey and the horses picked their way carefully through the narrow channel tunnel and we were faced by the magnificent Treasury. It wasn't a building as Petra was carved out of solid rock so this place was magnificent. It was used in the Indiana Jones film with Harrison Ford. The top of the Treasury was carved with an urn and many believed that it contained treasure and had tried to shoot it open as the bullet marks confirmed. We entered the door and found ourselves in a huge room but as there was nothing else to examine we left to tour the rest of the city.

We couldn't do much in a day, but our guide explained the watering system and showed us most of the sites. There were Bedouins wandering around and apparently it was quite common to find a coin or other artefact but I'm afraid we were not so lucky.

We returned the way we had come and we were dropped at the airfield in Maan to await the Arab Legion plane. After half an hour a Land Rover roared up in a cloud of dust and a Queen's Bays officer jumped out to tell us he'd had a call and the plane would be late so he invited us to his Mess to have a drink until it arrived. We accepted as we didn't know how long it would be and there was no place to wait. We arrived at his Mess and he said we could have stayed with them instead of in the hotel. As they had had a party that night and the evidence was on the walls we thought we had probably been better off in the hotel. I don't know though it would have been another experience!

Christmas was fast approaching and there were the usual parties, dances. We thought it would be lovely to go to the Church of Nativity in Bethlehem sometime in the season so we approached Father Hoad. As we weren't Roman Catholics he couldn't obtain a service in the Church but he could arrange for us to go to a service in the Shepherd's field so we opted for that. As it happened no one went to Bethlehem as there were riots and it was out of bounds.

Both Maggie and I had such a lot of hospitality from the families that when we sat down to write a list of people to invite to our drinks party prior to the New Year's Eve fancy dress ball in the Mess, we found that nearly everyone in the camp was on our list, so we posted a notice in the Mess hall to say the teachers were inviting all officers and their families to drinks on New Year's Eve.

Now that was a lot of people, so the day before, December 30th, James a teacher and a few fellows came down and mixed drinks in buckets, clean ones of course. There was a brandy sour, a gin-bound concoction and whisky and soda. Naturally they tasted them all to get the right mixture, so by the end of evening they were plastered but they had already promised they would remain sober at the party so they could serve the drinks and then when they arrived at the dance they celebrate then.

The drinks were ready so on the morning of the 31st we got the flat prepared. Now my bedroom had two doors, one led to the hall and the other to the lounge. So the obvious thing to do was take my bed down and remove it and some of the furniture to Maggie's room, so people could move round, bedroom, lounge, hall and dining room and we reckoned this way we could accommodate them all. A table was put in the kitchen across the doorway and this served as a bar.

Everything was prepared and the guests in their fancy dresses arrived. They were various and wonderful. In the flat below, the OD Padre had returned home to the UK. The new inhabitants were a lovely family and the husband was a great character. His wife had fancied a harem outfit and he had had one made especially for her. It had baggy diaphanous trousers and a beautiful top and she looked lovely.

As people arrived and the drinks flowed, the place filled up; fortunately we had removed all carpets so the odd spillage and cigarette ash on the floor didn't matter. It was a successful party and eventually everyone left and made their way to the camp. Judy in the lovely harem outfit made her way to her own flat where she spent the night feeling the effect of too many cocktails so she missed the dance.

Maggie and I hadn't had much to drink at our party but when we got to the Mess we danced and drank and had a wonderful time.

After celebrating the start of the New Year 1956 and winding down the evening until well into the morning, my partner and I wandered back to the flat. As we passed the downstairs apartment the door opened and the sergeant's wife asked us to enter as her first foot. Everyone was in a happy mood but not drunk by any means. She offered us a whisky to toast the New Year and although I thought, 'But I've been drinking gin all evening,' I had had enough to make me feel – well one more won't make any difference; so I drank it. We didn't stay long enough to have another which I would certainly have refused and then we wandered upstairs to put the flat to rights.

First I had to get my bed out of Maggie's room and the two of us lugged it from her room to across the lounge and into my room. With great effort we put it together and got the bedclothes on.

At this point I felt ill too ill to get to the bathroom. "I feel sick get me a bucket from the kitchen. I lay on the bed not daring to move. Bill found a bucket and I was sick. Oh was I sick!! After a while when I felt a little better Bill left and I fell asleep.

Next morning I still felt awful and just couldn't get out of bed. Maggie asked if I wanted anything but the only thing I wanted was to be left alone.

Later in the morning all the lads who had helped us to prepare for our cocktail party came to help clear up and put the flat to rights. I still couldn't move but eventually Maggie came to me and said I had to get up as it wasn't fair for everyone else to do the work. I staggered out of bed and asked what I could do. We were having pork for lunch so she said, "Baste the pork."

I took it out of the oven but the smell was nauseating and I must have turned green. The lads all laughed and shouted, "Get back to bed." I did and stayed there until the following morning where, feeling much better, I got up to go to work. School started on January 2nd and after a quiet morning I went to the Mess for lunch. My arrival was greeted with shouts of "What happened to New Year's Day?" and other ribald comments but by this time I felt back to normal and thanked them all for their help in making our party a success.

I enjoyed teaching in Amman. The school was on the camp and very close to the runway used by 249 Squadron with their Venom fighters. The CO's son was in my class he always referred to them as, "My daddy's planes."

We used to sing that song, 'Down at the railway station early in the morning, see the little choo choo trains all in a row'. I added another verse.

Down at the aerodrome early in the morning
See the little Venoms all in a row

See the little plot pull the little joy stick

Weee – off we go.

One of the mothers came to see me about her little boy. She was Irish and she was having trouble getting her son to bed at night. He would not go and she wondered if I would come to her quarters one night and tell him to go to bed and stay there.

I didn't feel I could do that but I said I'd have a word with him. He was a lovely little lad and after school I asked him to stay behind and I explained that he needed his sleep and it would be better for him if he went to bed, had a little read then settled down to sleep.

Much to my surprise it worked and a while later his mother came to school to thank me and said, "I know you will receive your reward in heaven."

Half term arrived and a trip to Damascus was arranged. The coach left on Saturday and returned on Sunday night, but on Saturday a party had been arranged at one of the pilot's and his wife's home and I decided I'd rather go to that. Maggie went on the trip and I asked her to buy me a silver necklace, chunky and in the form of leaves encircling my neck. She wasn't enthusiastic, but a pilot officer standing nearby said he would get me one.

The party was a great success. Two of the lads played Chug-a-lug and the others chanted encouragement. The game consists of players with a pint of beer in front of them. They shout Chug-a-lug and then down the pint in one long swallow. The first to slam his empty glass on the table is the winner. Of course the loser demands a re-match and they do it again.

The two combatants in this case had drunk two pints and with honours even a third was called for. Before they could start, Pete shouted, "Just a minute, I need to hurl," and he dashed out, was sick and then returned to carry on the challenge.

After the buffet I returned to my flat to bring a book I had promised to a friend. I was wearing a dress, purchased from Eva in Nicosia which was very fashionable and trendy at the time. It had a very full skirt, cut on the cross and the bodice was off the shoulder and fastened down the back.

When we got to the flat I suggested to my escort that I change the dress so that it fastened down the front and we'd see if anyone noticed. On our return, in spite of their merriment they noticed immediately and we got a lot of ribbing but it added to the fun.

I got the necklace from the PO and although it wasn't as I had envisaged it was chunky, silver and I still enjoyed wearing it.

The son of one of the teachers was at boarding school in Bethlehem. On the camp we only taught up to age 11 so older children went to a boarding school either in Jordan or the UK. She asked me to accompany them on his return to school, so that I could see the, "Little Town." I felt I would rather go for a longer visit but Maggie who had already been, persuaded me to go and I'm glad I did as no other opportunity arose.

We travelled in a taxi driven by Abraham. There were few taxis allowed on the camp but Abraham was everyone's favourite driver. Apart from being a good driver he was fun and a pleasant companion.

Before taking John to his boarding school Abraham took us to the manger square and we went inside the Church of the Nativity. In my mind's eye I had imagined the scene of the birth but this was not the same. We went downstairs into an area with lights in a sort of alcove. Even so it was full of atmosphere and with my imagination working overtime I had a sense of the area hundreds of years ago.

The bell over the Church is only rung at Christmas. It was tied to the side of the building, but we passed it as we climbed the spiral staircase to the top of the tower to view the area. As we passed it I couldn't resist giving it a flick with my fingers so I can now say I rang the Christmas bell.

It was a flying visit but most enjoyable and as I didn't go back to Bethlehem I was very glad of the opportunity to visit it even for a few hours.

At half term we had a letter from Liz, who had been in Abyad with us, in Cyprus to ask if she could visit us for the holiday. Unfortunately we had arranged a visit to Habbaniyah in Iraq but we told her she was welcome to come and stay at our flat.

She accepted and we saw her before we set off for our holiday. We showed her around the place and instructed her in the art of lighting the heater. It was still cold in Jordan and we had rented this heater for a few of the winter months. It was quite an object, but it did heat the place once we got it working. It was about three feet high with a silver ball at the side and with a pipe joining it to the main heater. The ball was fitted with paraffin and when a few drops were allowed to drip into the main cylinder a lighted paper on metal was dropped through the little door which was then shut quickly. With a bit of luck it ignited the paraffin and hey presto a wonderful warmth permeated the room. If you didn't have a bit of luck it could take a long time to ignite.

When we returned from our holiday we found Liz had not had luck and the carpet was sodden with paraffin. It's a wonder she hadn't caused a fire but summer was coming and with it the hot weather and no harm was done, apart from the carpet which wasn't expensive.

Having settled her in the flat Maggie and I set off for Iraq. We were cadging a lift on a cargo plane taking goods from Cyprus up country and calling in at Amman and Habbaniyah.

The two pilots were very friendly fun-loving chaps and before we set off they asked us how we were getting back. We said we'd hitch a lift and they said that could be difficult as there wasn't always a flight available but they said they were due back in three days and they would give us a lift if the officer in charge at Habb said there wasn't room they wouldn't take his cargo and as there was always a backlog of cargo he would have to let us travel with them. Blackmail; I don't think they liked the man in charge at Habbaniyah and we soon found out why.

We landed and joined a whole room of passengers and a sergeant major was trying to sort out who was going where. Eventually he shouted "All those going to Amman stand there." Half the people moved out to where he pointed. "All those going up country stand there," and he pointed to the other side of the room and the rest of the passengers went there. That left Maggie and I in the middle of the room and he looked at us as if we were morons.

"Are you going to Amman?"

"No."

"Then you are going up country?"

"No."

"Well where are you going?"

"Here, we've come for a holiday."

No one had ever gone to Habb for a holiday.

"Where are you staying?"

"We don't know."

His face was a picture, but eventually everything was sorted out and we ended up in the Officers' Club.

We met two of the officers who had spent a short time in Amman. They wanted us to go to a ball but we hadn't evening dresses with us and although they arranged for two of the wives to lend us dresses we declined and said we'd have an early night.

At two in the morning there was banging on the door. We wondered what was happening but our two friends had left the dance and come to visit us complete with a bottle of spirits. They were quite tipsy but we had a merry time until the next door people banged on the walls so our party broke up.

We spent a lot of time at the swimming pool and the first time I dived in it was so cold I couldn't get my breath for quite a while. I don't know where the water came from but it was very cold.

We had intended to go to Bagdad but didn't get round to it so after a few days rest we once again arrived at the airport.

The RAF was very good to its civilian workers and if there was room on a plane they would take them up. We could go anywhere – Hong Kong, Singapore, anywhere their planes went – BUT if they didn't have a place when you wanted to return you had to pay your own fare on a civil airplane so that you were back on duty where you were supposed to be.

I don't think civilian planes flew into Habb but even so we were very pleased to have come to an arrangement with our pals who had brought us and we boarded their plane for Amman.

As we reached Amman we were told the undercarriage wouldn't go down so we had to circle round until the petrol was used up and they would crash land. Why is it when you're going you don't believe anything bad can happen to you?

We went round and round and they were just telling us what to do when they managed to get the undercarriage down. We landed safely and we got off the plane Maggie took out her cigarettes and was about to light one when Dave shouted "For God's sake don't light that." Apparently there was quite a lot of fuel around.

We thanked them for an interesting flight and made our way back to the flat and the soggy carpet.

1956 was a leap year and according to custom if a lady asked a man to marry her on February 29th and he declined he had to buy her a pair of gloves. On February 29th I arrived in the Mess and the first man I met was Jim, one of the teachers, so I asked him if he'd marry me.

"Yes" came the reply so I knew there were no gloves coming from him.

The next one on my right was Will; "Will you marry me?"

Again I got the reply, "Yes just name the day."

My plan wasn't working very well. Next came Mike but this time to my questions came the reply "No." I think he thought I might be serious. "Right you owe me a pair of gloves." By now I think the others were aware of my little game so we had a laugh and that was the end.

Well not quite because when Mike went to Malta on an exercise he returned with lace dressing table mats which he said were instead of gloves.

As the warm weather came, the hills around us began to show a haze of green. Each day we walked to work the hills had a deeper green, spring had arrived.

Remembering what I had been told at Mafraq when I arrived in Jordan, that come Spring the dust would turn to a sea of flowers and that under one foot would be six different types of wild flower, we decided to visit Jerash the Roman town but to picnic first in the Forest of Ajlan.

Four of us hired Abraham for the day and Maggie and I packed a picnic hamper and on a beautiful Sunday we set out.

The forest was beautiful and the flowers were varied and many. We had our picnic which included tinned asparagus. Everyone raved about it, but as I hadn't ever tasted it before I had one or two stalks decided it was nothing to get excited about and left the rest of the lunch.

We packed up and journeyed to Jerash which certainly held up to our expectation. It was amazing to think that it had been built hundreds of years earlier and yet the plan of the town was easily seen. We walked down the main street and I had my photograph taken sitting in a large bowl. It would have been nice to have had a guide to explain things to us but it was a lovely day, and we were the only ones there and we explored and thoroughly enjoyed ourselves.

Eventually we piled back into the car and headed for home.

As we came nearer to Amman I felt queasy and realised I was not going to make it back to the flat. Abraham stopped the car and I was ill. Asparagus – I shall never eat it again and I couldn't wait to get back home.

By next morning I was fine and after work when I walked to the Mess the C of E padre asked if I was alright. He had been in a car which had passed us on the road, just as I was being sick, I assured him I was fine and thought – no matter where you go someone you know will be around.

Every Saturday night Maggie and I went to the Mess and chatted and drank and some nights if it was quiet we would all adjourn to our flat. One particular night a crowd of us decided to leave the bar and after collecting a few bottles we walked down the road to our apartment. We invited Jim our school colleague and his roommate, the C of E Padre and one of the pilots whom I didn't know very well. He had been playing rugby and soccer that afternoon and because he was tired he had asked the MO for some sort of a pill to get him through the afternoon. Now, we were all relaxing in the flat.

The fellows, not the padre played chug a lug for a while, we got the dice out and played liar dice and all the time we filled the glass. We were certainly not drunk but we were very merry. Jimmy, as usual fell into a deep sleep so for a bit of fun, Maggie and I got out our makeup and painted his face – lipstick rouge, shadow, etc., the garish lot.

We thought it hilarious until someone wanted to go to the toilet and the door was locked. No one answered the knock and we realised our pilot friend was missing and obviously locked in the lavatory. After a long time we eventually aroused him and he opened the door and then collapsed on the settee. He was unconscious and looked awful.

We realised we had to get the MO quickly. The Padre said it was now Sunday and he shouldn't be here and he left. A crowd thought it wouldn't look good to see Jimmy in that condition so they roused him and walked him back as quickly as possible.

Maggie and I and a couple of fairly sober friends were left. We told the Sergeant and his wife who lived near us to leave as we didn't want anything awful on his CV and we waited for the doctor.

He arrived with an ambulance in about half an hour and by that time Ron was beginning to come round and wonder where he was. The doctor ordered him to be taken back to camp and insisted he got on a stretcher. He protested he could walk but the medic wasn't taking any chances and insisted he got him into the ambulance. He was recovering quite quickly by now and as they pushed him into the ambulance he stood up and said, "You know if you'd gone to bed with me, Jean, this would never have happened." The two orderlies stared at me and the doctor glared and stood open mouthed; I thought of protesting but decided against it and the ambulance sped off.

We returned to the flat, quietly cleared up and went to bed.

Next morning on the door of our flat was a notice which was headed:

Abandon Hope all ye who enter here.

Then followed with illustrations all the dire things which could happen to anyone foolish to visit us!

It was Granville and Sue our neighbours who were obviously quite artistic who had pinned it to the door and we had a good laugh but we didn't leave it there, we bought it inside and showed it, to our visitors but it didn't put them off!

The lady who lived in the bottom flat, the one who had given me a hefty scotch on Hogmanay was expecting a baby. She already had a much loved little daughter Fiona aged about three and she was worried how Fiona would react to a new baby.

She and her husband prepared for the birth and when they Dad and Fiona went to bring his wife and new baby home the new baby was in a carry cot and next to it was a small carry cot containing a doll. They explained the large one was Mummy's and the small one was Fiona's and they all went home happily, Daddy carrying his son and Fiona carrying her "new baby."

Whenever Mother fed or bathed baby, Fiona did the same with her doll.

This worked very happily until one day Mum was having a nap in the chair when the door opened and there stood Fiona with her doll under one arm and the real baby tucked under the other arm. He was screaming and Fiona marched up to her mother and thrust her brother at her and said "Here, yours is crying."

Fortunately no harm was done and the new family thrived, although I wonder if Fiona even realised her baby didn't grow as Mummy's did.

Many visitors came to RAF Amman, people to do with working with aircraft. I met one man who knew of my brother who worked at Bristol Aircraft Factory although they had never met. There was usually some cocktail party for them and we were always invited.

At one of these receptions Maggie was getting on well with one of the reps, and I was socialising with the fellows I knew.

At the end we wandered home, I opened the door and prepared for bed, then the bell rang and I walked to the door to answer it, but Maggie whispered to me to stop. I looked at her but she cautioned me to be quiet and we tiptoed to the door. There were two fellows outside and one was saying, "I'm sure she said it was this flat, ring again." They rang and knocked, but eventually left, but then they stood outside the block of flats and shouted up, "Maggie, are you there?"

Fortunately they left Amman the next day so we didn't see them, but I wondered what she had been saying to them in fun, but which they had taken seriously. She never told me but I had a pretty good idea!

The pilots flew their little Venoms over Jordan and they would take off and land near the school but I don't remember them ever disturbing us.

There was only one time when there was excitement, when one of the engines began to fail and it wasn't possible to land safely. The pilots were always told it cost more to train them than an aircraft's value, so always bail out and save yourself.

Thomas was in just such a position and radioed, "Flare our flare out" and he was told to parachute out and ditch the aircraft in a safe spot. The other pilots heard him of course and Peter radioed and said "Don't go yet Thomas wait till I get near, I want to see you jump!" Thomas jumped and landed safely and the event was the topic of conversation in the bar that night.

After "The Little Hut" in Abyad I was keen to join any Dramatic Society that was around. There was talk of doing Julius Caesar with some of the Embassy crowd in Amman and performing it in one of the Roman ruins in Amman but nothing came of it. We planned to meet to discuss it but the idea never left the ground. I did enjoy my Amateur Dramatics and I suppose when I had the choice of RAF locations after leaving Egypt I should have tried to go to a station with a thriving society but it never crossed my mind that any station would not have an Amateur Dramatic Society. The one in Abyad had been so big and had produced plays from 1949 with *See How They Run* and in 1953 they had produced three plays *Little Lambs Eat Ivy*, *We Proudly Present*, and *Night Must Fall*. Of course there were some fine actors and actresses many who could have worked in a West End theatre.

The Little Hut was my swan song as I never 'trod the boards' again. Still it was nice to go out on a high note!

We did get an invitation from the Embassy to a garden party. I debated whether we should wear hats and carry gloves. The decision was all very light-hearted and we decided to wear a smart cotton dress and as our legs were brown we wouldn't wear stockings. Will and Mike were escorting us. Will had a car but when we told them we were going bare-legged they refused to take us. I thought they were joking, but no, we had to make our own way there whilst they went by car. Anyway we met at the garden party and they must have decided we looked quite smart because they brought us back. Well it saved us the taxi fare.

One Sunday morning we had an unexpected caller. An officer informed us that under no circumstance had we to leave our flat that day or in the future until we were told we could. Naturally we asked why but he repeated "Do not leave the flat under any circumstances until I say." When he left we wondered on the circumstances that meant we had to be homebound.

Later in the evening as we settled to write letters home as we usually did on Sundays we could hear gun shots echoing all-round the hills. It was a beautiful evening and we knew the Arabs often celebrated by firing guns into the air, but after our warning this sound appeared much more sinister. There was a knock at the door and Jimmy appeared. We asked how he had got out of camp and he replied as he was a civilian he didn't consider himself subject to forces orders! We asked what was going on but he didn't know either. We were glad of his company and after a pleasant evening he returned to camp.

The next day, Monday, we were told we could return to school but no one seemed to know what the fuss had been about. Just before playtime Maggie came into my classroom and said "Read this." It was a child's diary of the weekend, her father was an air traffic controller and her entry read "This weekend Daddy has been very busy because Glubb Pasha had to leave Amman very quickly."

Now we knew the reason why we had been “confined to barracks” but there were no repercussions and life went on as normal.

We were planning a weekend in Jerusalem but having a day free decided to pay a day visit. Once again we got Abraham to taxi us there and of course he proved an excellent guide. In 1956 there were few visitors and it was easy to move around in the city. We visited many of the places and in most of them we were the only visitors; The Via Dolorosa with the Statue of the Cross, the Garden of Gethsemane the Dome of the Rock, the lovely little Pater Noster Church with the Lord’s Prayer in many languages.

It was a lovely day, hot in Jericho (where the walls came tumbling down) and a visit to the Dead Sea where I decided on a longer visit, I would swim, so that I, too, could lie back and read a newspaper like everyone else did.

Unfortunately I didn’t return to the Dead Sea to read a newspaper and I didn’t return to Jerusalem for my weekend.

Whilst we were there Abraham pointed out the modern part of Jerusalem which ‘belonged’ to Israel. Now of course it’s all in Israelis hands. I haven’t been back but pictures I have seen since either from tourists, where everywhere is so crowded or from the news where everyone seems intent on blowing everything and everybody up, tends me to believe that I saw it at the right time and I have no desire to return, not even to swim in the Dead Sea.

Our flat was in a lovely position and as we were on the second floor we had a good view over the hills surrounding Amman. I was told that we were on the side of the valley where David and Goliath met. I didn’t know if it was true but I like to believe it was.

It was only a short walk up a hill to the camp and half way up was the guard house. We became well known to the guards and never had any difficulty passing them.

Chatting one night in the flat one of the lads mentioned that if someone was going into town they could obtain a condom at the guard house. I laughed because I thought they were joking.

"It's true and you get a little tube with it."

"A tube of what for what?" I asked.

"To use after you've used the condom."

I couldn't believe this and Maggie and I decided they were pulling our legs.

Next night, Ted arrived with a little brown paper packet closed with a pin.

"There, you," he said, "have a look but don't lose the pin!"

I opened it and sure enough there was a condom and little tube.

"Don't forget the pin," he said.

"Why?"

"It's to pierce the tube, stupid, otherwise how would you be able to get the ointment out?"

Condoms also had another use out there. Well of course they had but I mean yet another use. The pilots put them over the guns of the Venoms to keep the sand out. Apparently they were just the right size. Of course they could have been teasing me but it does seem a good idea and certainly the sand got everywhere.

One evening in the bar there was a new face; Ted and the new man were sitting in the corner and Ted shouted across, "Meet the girl with the best legs in the Middle East." The newcomer couldn't find out if this was true because I was sitting up at the bar. He was an army officer who was in charge of the Army Postal unit and he was based in Agaba but came to Amman to do spot checks.

We were introduced by name, 'instead of legs', and at that moment a crowd of pilots who had been to a party rolled in. They were quite merry and one who had perhaps had more than the others shouted "Here am I the fairy queen, farting and belching and heavy with child." I happened to glance at the army officer's face and he was furious. He didn't approve of such language especially in front of a lady. The incident passed and we enjoyed a pleasant evening.

The next day Maggie and I were early for lunch and as I went to sit in the ante room the punka fans blew my skirt up. It was a mid-calf circular skirt, which was fashionable then and the whole thing billowed up exposing my nether regions. The 'postman', Ken, who was sitting opposite said, "Lovely legs and I see they go all the way to the top." We got talking and when I realised the Amman Postal Unit was under his command I told him I had a complaint about it.

I explained that we bought many things from the UK mainly records and beauty products and when they arrived at the PO we had to collect them personally. As the PO was open only during the school hours we normally sent a child at playtime to collect our parcels. The Sergeant in charge refused to give them to a child and said we had to collect them personally. We tried to explain we couldn't leave school but he was adamant, "So, Ken, what could you do about it?"

He said he would sort it out and he did so I invited him down to the flat for a drink.

That evening he went into the bar with Ted and said, casually, "I was invited to the teachers' flat for a drink, but I don't know where it is so I'm not going."

"Don't be silly all you have to do is go to the taxi rank and ask for the teachers' flat in fact I'll come with you."

So the two of them turned up and the next day Ken left for Agaba.

The British Forces Post Office is an essential part of service life. It is a terrific morale booster unless it is delivering a Dear John letter. It is surprising the things that are sent by parcel. One lad had said how he missed Mum's Sunday roast dinner so she sent him one including the gravy which was a sorry mess when it arrived.

One day Ken was in the bar when the CO entered and asked why he looked so glum. "The mail plane has been grounded so I can't get the post to Agaba."

The CO was a typical 40s RAF officer with handlebar moustache and a very cheery disposition, well to us anyway. "We can't have that," he shouted, "get the mail and I'll take you in my Pembroke."

Everything was loaded and on the flight south the CO said, "Let's have a quick look at Petra," and he flew the little plane down into the Rose Red City for a quick recce.

Ken, not the best of travellers, felt his stomach had left his body but he survived to land in Agaba and distribute the mail.

The CO had the nickname 'Drains' I never found out why but it was something that had happened at a previous posting.

He couldn't have been a very old and had a charming wife and a little boy who ended up in my class. I don't know what he was like as a leader but he seemed on good terms with the pilots. He was always on about a party and once in a very crowded bar I had a drink sent over to him. When the barman gave him it and said it was from me he raised his glass and shouted out, "Cheers to the mistress." It caused a laugh but we were used to it.

My contract with the RAF was for three years and was supposed to end Easter 1956 but I extended it until July to finish the school year. Maggie's contract also ended then so we set off back to the UK. Mike was already in the UK so Will was the only one who arrived at the plane to see us off. We had said our goodbyes to the others at various farewell parties. Will give us each a hug and a kiss, wished us bon voyage and we climbed aboard the plane and set off for Cyprus where we had an overnight stay.

Liz was still working there and had arranged an early outing for us. She arrived in an army vehicle with her RAF boyfriend and two others for Maggie and me. Mine was an army officer. They were equipped with guns and we went to a night club.

This wasn't the Cyprus I knew and loved. Men with guns an army vehicle and the nightclub was surrounded with barbed wire and guards!

It was a pleasant evening but not as carefree as my former visits. Liz had had one terrifying experience she had gone to a restaurant with a friend and as the window seats were occupied they had taken a table at the back. A bomb had been thrown through the window killing those near the window and she and her friend had dived underneath the table and escaped from the debris which was everywhere.

She realised how lucky she had been but it left her nervous and careful of the places she visited.

The next day we left for the UK. Maggie went to a job in the south and I went back to Richmond and started in September at a school in Catterick Camp. I had worked there before so I knew what to expect and in one of the classes was a little girl I had taught in Amman. I think she found it hard to adjust.

At least the winter wasn't as bad as my previous time there in 1950. Then even the ink in the ink wells had frozen and we sat in winter coats, hats and gloves. The army authorities wouldn't allow us to close the school as most of the parents were working and the children would have no one to look after them. I ended up with yellow jaundice but at least I was warm in bed.

My social life was not exciting either I went to some dances or out for dinner but television was now in about every house and sometimes ruled what time you met.

My father was Mayor that year and he and Mum had an invitation to a garden party at Buckingham Palace. They were allowed to take one daughter, me, but I had to be vetted. The Town Clerk assured the authorities that I was of suitable character and not divorced. So the Palace was something to look forward to.

We travelled to London in the mayoral car which parked in the Mall whilst we went into the Palace Gardens for tea and cakes. Not having been to the Palace before I had a good look round as I walked from the 'front door' to the garden.

The 'peers of the realm' arranged lanes through which a member of the Royal Family would walk. Various people were brought forward to be introduced to the royal. We chose Prince Philip's lane and just in front of us was someone who was to be presented so Philip stopped very close to us so we had a good view. He was smaller than I imagined but so good looking. He and the Queen made a very handsome couple.

They reckon that when you go to a garden party you would always see someone you knew. As we stood sipping tea from bone china cups the boy who had lived in the pub next door rushed by. He was in uniform and had been a Battle of Britain pilot. He was obviously in a hurry so we didn't stop him.

When it was time to leave we walked to the front of the palace and a servant called on the tannoy, "The Mayor of Richmond's car," and George came out of the parking area picked us up and we returned home.

So, back to civilisation, life albeit it was teaching in a school on Catterick Camp; the class was a mixture of army children and a few civilians. They were 11 year olds and looking forward to leaving and going to the big school."

My social life was different. Most of my friends had left and I went to dances I was considered an "expensive bird" because I drank gin and lime. I went with my mother and father to various functions and visited my friends in different parts of the country but I missed the community life and the winter seemed very harsh after my three years in the sun.

Christmas and New Year were wonderful but after that I began to get itchy feet and seeing an advertisement for teachers in Germany I decided to apply. This time I had my RAF reference to accompany my others and I was invited to an interview in London.

I arrived with the other hopefuls and was summoned before two Army officers for my interview. To my surprise they were least interested in asking me the usual questions one expected.

"You were in Amman when Glubb Pasha left, what was it like?"

Of course this was just after the Suez Crisis so the Middle East was once again in the news.

I told them of my experience and they asked if I wanted to ask them anything.

I said I would prefer to work in an RAF school if that was possible. All the schools in Germany were administered by the army so they said they would see what they could do.

When I returned home I began to wonder if the RAF had any vacancies in any other part of the world. I wrote to them quoting my reference number and received the reply that they had a two year vacancy in Aden if I was interested.

Aden! Now that would be quite hot but it was only for two years so yes I would go, I wrote to the Army and told them to forget my application for Germany I was off to Aden with the RAF.

I knew my mother in particular was upset at my going. My father always said, "I have had my life you go and enjoy yours."

As I was going to London to shop for clothes I took Mum with me and as she loved Norman Wisdom I thought I'd treat her to his show at the Palladium. I rang up but they only had seats in the Stalls and they were expensive so I refused them

After a while when we were having coffee I thought – you miserable mean thing, here you are going away for two years and you won't even treat your Mum to something she'd love, so I got back on the phone and reserved two seats.

We collected them at the Box Office and were shown to our seats. I always take a newspaper to read until the curtain goes up and heard my mother say, "I think your friend is over there he's waving to you." The reply, "Oh it's only one of my fans." I looked at her neighbour and it was Arthur Askey. He was with his wife and Jimmy Jewel and his wife, and my mother spent the interval passing programmes from the audience for them to sign. It made her weekend and I was so pleased my generosity had overcome my meanness.

Easter holidays and once again I made my way to Hendon to meet with all the other people who were flying to Aden. I looked around for another woman but there were none. Everybody on the plane apart from the air hostess was male. I was the only female passenger among all the other RAF personnel. Very nice, I found I had the ladies powder room all to myself.

It was going to be a long journey as we were not able to fly via Egypt. After the Suez crisis planes going to Aden had to go the long route. First stop was Malta where we stayed the night. On the plane I was sitting next to a squadron leader called Paddy so we had got quite friendly. I was sitting with him at breakfast when he said "I think someone is looking for you." I looked up. Mike was striding towards me. 249 Squadron was stationed in Malta and he came to take me for a car ride until it was time to board the plane for the next step. We drove to someplace on the coast – not far as Malta is such a small island and then it was back to the airport for the next step.

This was very short, just across the sea to Idris in North Africa so we could take on fuel for the next stop which was Kano in Nigeria.

At Idris we got off the plane whilst it refuelled and many made their way to the bar to get a drink, then they all drifted back to their seats minus hard liquor but some had cups of tea. It seems the price of the hard stuff was high and people decided to wait until they were airborne again.

We landed in Kano in the night and whilst the plane once again refuelled we had the customary meal of egg and chips. As we emerged into the night air we could hear the insects chirping and the night sky was full of stars. It was cool and pleasant but we hadn't long to admire it before we were once again on the plane for the next stop.

We landed in the Belgian Congo once again to refuel and sat on a veranda drinking coffee next to Belgians who eyed us with curiosity; then on the Entebbe where once again we were to spend the night.

We had dinner in the hotel and I went to bed as there didn't seem to be anything else to do I just got settled when there was a knock at my door and I was handed a message. "Come on get ready we're going out on to the town."

Quickly I put on my glad rags and joined some of the others to go out and find some night life. We didn't find much but it was better than sleeping and eventually we all made our way back to the hotel to prepare ourselves for the last laps of the journey.

As we were nearing Aden the air hostess pointed to a 'barometer' on the cabin wall and said "Watch that rise it's the humidity bulb." When we landed it was obvious this place would be hot and humid.

It wasn't too bad but as I was wearing a suit and the others were in their RAF blues I think we soon realised we could be more suitably dressed.

I was met by an Education Officer and taken to a Civilian Officer's Mess which was between RAF Khormaksar and Aden. It was on the main road called Ma'alla Strait and all civilian officers,' teachers, air traffic controllers, were billeted there. It consisted of three air conditioned buildings.

Once again these were long low single storey buildings. The top one was the bar, mess and kitchen and a spur each side men on one side and women on the other. I was allocated a room and introduced to the other teachers and then that evening before dinner I met some of the men over a drink prior to dinner.

Ma'alla Mess was mid-way between Khormaksar and Aden town and they were joined by a straight duel carriageway. Further past Aden was Tarshyne which was another Mess for service men. The Khormaksur mess had eight Squadron stationed there and the junior school was also in its compound.

Further on still was Little Aden. This was the BP Oil area and all the workers and families lived there. It was about 20 miles from Aden along a causeway and you knew when you were nearly there as Flossie would be burning brightly. This was the flame that burns over a refinery.

One of our teachers had married an oil man and had a little air-conditioned bungalow; we visited her occasionally but we didn't see much social activity but I suppose plenty of events would be organised for the people who lived there.

At the other end of Aden was the Officer's Club with beach, restaurant, and bar, swimming pool and Squash courts and even further on was Gold Mohur which was a club for all personnel whether service or civilian.

A bus picked us up to take us to and from work and it soon became obvious that a car was a necessity if one wanted to enjoy all the amenities of the area. I heard about a squadron leader who was going home to the UK, and had a little Fiat Topolino for sale. He had bought it new and it was about a year old so I parted with £80 and became the proud owner of ADN247 It was very small and the hood was permanently down, after all it rained only once in the two years I was out there. It had two seats but there was a ledge in the back so it could hold four. It was wonderful, it took me to work and play and I was very popular as other teachers didn't even drive never mind own a car.

The Civilian Officers' Mess in Ma'alla was quite popular with other civilians living in Aden. Among the visitors were the Eagles Airways Crews. Eagle Airways had the contract for taking service personnel from Aden to Kenya for holidays. Although Aden had the sun, sea and sand it was a bit hot and it was lovely to get away to Kenya to the coolness of Nairobi or the rains in the rainy season and the holiday places in Mombasa. And of course there were the game parks and safaris. So the Eagle Airway ferried the holiday makers on Friday for their two week break and they returned back to Aden on Sunday.

I got quite friendly with them and one of the pilots Gerry suggested I flew with them for the weekend, out on Friday back on Sunday. They had a spare seat on the plane so provided I got permission from the RAF movement's people I could have a pleasant weekend break.

Thinking it was purely a formality I asked the RAF officer if I could go.

"No."

He didn't seem to have any real reason for refusal but he was adamant that he would not give me permission to go. He must have got out of the wrong side of the bed that day because nothing I said would make him change his mind.

I returned to Gerry and said I was sorry I couldn't go. He went to the Captain in charge of Eagle Airways who said, "Tell her she can come as supernumerary crew." So I went as an air hostess.

I served a few meals but when one of the proper air hostesses said, "Whatever you do, don't fall against that door." The door in question was the main door into the aircraft. When I asked why she said it was a bit dodgy so I quietly sat down and left them to it. She was joking.

We landed in Mombasa and had a very nice hotel by the sea or ocean I should say. The weather was perfect, the food good and with the palm trees and stars it was very romantic. To think all this was free and it was a lovely break from the heat of work.

Work! Well of course that was my reason for being in Aden. The school on Khormaksar was fairly small. At first there had been just one school for all children but as the numbers had grown they had split them into senior and junior. The headmaster Mr Rice had opted to be the Head of the junior so another head was needed for the Secondary School in Tarshyne.

The children as in Egypt and Jordan were at various stages and as usual some bright children who had missed the basics through moving around were being held back. I applied the techniques of the good old phonetic Beacon system and it was lovely to see such improvements in a very short time.

The social life was quite good. apart from parties there was the Officers' Club at Gold Mohur.

There was a dance at the Officers' Club because it was hot; a 'floor' was rigged on the beach. It was very pleasant to hear the water lapping the shore and the band playing for the dancers who were getting hot and sticky cavorting to the music.

Very nice until my partner who had recently come on leave from Up Country, caught his sandal (very informal these do's) under my big toe nail which of course was long and beautifully painted. It really hurt and I limped across to the cloakrooms and hoisted my foot into the basin.

The blood (and sand) was spurting out to the rhythm of my heartbeat and I tried to dance some more but when I left a trail of blood I thought it time to retire.

Eventually I went to the doctor and when it still didn't clear up after treatment he thought the best thing to do was remove the toe nail.

I went to his surgery during playtime and with a local anaesthetic he removed the nail and before he bandaged it up I asked if I could look at it. It didn't look any different from the other big toe as it was white but little beads of blood were starting to appear round the base; quite pretty really. He bandaged it and asked me what I was going to do. "Go back to work." I replied. He told me he thought I should get a taxi and return to my quarters and he would inform Mr Rice I wouldn't be returning to work just yet.

I couldn't feel anything and didn't know what all the fuss was about but I got a taxi and returned to Ma'alla. As I got out of the taxi I began to feel something in my toe. Within an hour it was quite painful and I was glad just to lie on my bed. Getting up to go to the toilet was agony and when the other teacher returned and started to tease me by putting their hands near my toe I could have killed her.

Within a short time I was mobile again but the daily dressings were unpleasant and of course there were no antibiotics or pain killers.

The Squadron changed places sometimes and 8th Squadron based in Aden changed with 249 now in Matta. It was quite a re-union and we swam at Gold Mohur and met up at various bars and it was nice to see them again but the visit was fleeting.

In the meantime Maggie had decided that work in England was boring so she contacted Air Ministry to see if they had any vacancy anywhere and they said they had Aden. She declined the offer as she didn't like too much heat and Egypt was fine from the climate point of view but definitely not Aden. They said they would keep her offer in mind and would contact her in a few weeks. Again they offered Aden and told her I was out there but she said that would not influence her accepting the job. However after a few more weeks she decided the heat and humidity of Aden was preferable to the British climate. She accepted the Air Ministry offer and arrived in Aden in time for the new term in September.

By this time we had decided the accommodation in Ma'alla Mess was poor and we wrote to Air Ministry to see if something better could be arranged. The only offer they suggested was that they gave us an accommodation allowance and we could determine our own living arrangements. Ma'alla Mess would still be our base and the mail and other communication would reach us there. So we moved out and went to stay in the Rock Hotel in the centre of Aden until we could find a flat. The Rock was quite a nice hotel for the time but we had to share three to a room which was not very nice and it was obvious the sooner we found a flat the better.

However finding a flat in Aden was not easy especially for three women. We had a contact, an Asian called Mr Shomas who was a great help. He found us a flat but when we went to the RAF Sergeant to get it vetted, he turned it down as not being suitable. We found out later that he himself had moved in with his family but by then it was too late to complain.

Mr Shomas invited us to his home for tea and to get to his room at the top of the house we passed through other rooms where some of his female family peeped out from behind curtains to look at the English women. I wonder what they thought of us with our bare legs and arms and heads uncovered.

We had tea with food of little crispy 'parcels.' With my 'delicate tummy' I declined the food saying I didn't eat between meals and later I asked Joan what it was like as she had tried it. "A bit like sand fried in batter but quite tasty."

Eventually Joan's boyfriend, a transport pilot, heard of a family going back to UK and he quickly stepped in to acquire the flat for the three of us. To seal the deal we had to go to Sheikh Othman to meet the owner Sir Maktari so the three of us arrived at his office to be met by him sitting behind a desk and his entourage on chairs round the office. All of them were in traditional robes.

Sir Maktari asked us various questions in a very quiet dignified manner and eventually said we could have the flat in the Maktari Buildings on Khormaksar beach. I then asked if we could have that in writing as we had had so many disappointments and been let down at the last minute so often. I think that question nearly lost us the flat. He looked me in the eye and very quietly said, "My word is my bond."

I felt an inch high. We thanked him and shortly afterwards we moved into the flat.

It was very nice. We were on the second floor and there were only four flats in the block two on the ground floor and two on the second floor and it consisted of a long lounge leading to a kitchen and off the middle of the lounge a door leading to a long corridor with three bedrooms and a bathroom leading off the side. We tossed for bedrooms; I was lucky and got the one on the front with a door leading to a balcony. Joan got the one at the back and Maggie got the small middle one with one window overlooking the side where the garages were.

All the floors were tiles for easy cleaning and we had a boy who came in and did for us. We couldn't get him to put the rugs straight along the tiles. They were always just a little bit off line. We asked him to lay them straight but his answer was, "Only God is perfect."

There was no boiler. The tanks were on the roof and the water was always hot.

We quickly settled in and got on surprisingly well. We worked in the morning, and went to the beach in the afternoon then did our school work and preparation, had a rest then went out somewhere in the evening; altogether a very pleasant existence.

School under Mr Rice was happy and the numbers fluctuated as always happens in RAF schools. We had such an influx in September that we didn't have enough classrooms and Mr Rice called a meeting to tell us what was happening.

A class was being set up in the Officers Mess in the billiard room which was huge. I was taking the remedial class so had the smallest class therefore I would move into the billiard room. The billiard room was next to the bar so I was told I couldn't keep nipping into the bar for the odd noggin. He was joking – I think!

So I moved into my classroom with my little brood and it was very pleasant. At playtime I had a drink (soft) sent in and apart from funny things on the blackboard most mornings and children finding unusual things in their desks, "Miss Hood I have a glass of dirty water in my desk" (gin and tonic) and when 249 Squadron were down I had some very funny notes and things left in my desk from my Amman friends, apart from that things went smoothly.

I heard that when 8 Squadron got merry some nights they went into the billiard room and sat at the desks and there was great hilarity but I never found out why.

As I have said I loved taking the remedial class in a RAF school because so many children who were behind academically were bright but had missed the early training usually through fathers being posted just as they were settling in their school.

All newcomers were sent to me and I tested their reading IQ and they were put into the appropriate class.

One little girl arrived and her reading was very poor so she was put in my class. Unfortunately her father was an officer in the EducatiON department and he didn't take kindly to his daughter being in my class and he contacted the head and they arrived at my desk.

I told him his daughter couldn't read and he said she could and he had heard her read. I asked if she read the proper words or did she substitute such things as jacket for coat, pussy for cat and he admitted she did. It was obvious she had learned the story by heart. It later transpired that she had been in a private school in Harrogate and when her father had been posted to Aden her mother had kept her at home until they had got a hiring and she could come out to live. The little girl had missed months of school so she stayed in my class and worked hard to catch up with her age group.

The school teachers regularly received invitations to cocktail parties held on ships. The crew were most hospitable and we enjoyed our visits.

One ship we were invited to had moved up outside the harbour line so we reached it in a speed boat. It was quite choppy but as the boat leapt the waves it was quite exhilarating. We reached the ship and it had been very firmly anchored to stop the swell. However it couldn't prevent a slight movement. Sacking had been put up round the drinks area to keep out the breeze and we made our way to the drinks area.

I began to feel queasy so only accepted a soft drink. A very nice sailor attached himself to me and he obviously saw my discomfort and suggested we left the sheltered area and found a perch near the rails with the breeze in our faces.

My friend was very good and entertaining. He was in is thirties and wasn't married and with lots of joking we decided we would marry if we met later and were still single. Needless to say I didn't see him again.

I was glad when the evening came to an end and as soon as I felt the motor boat leaping in the sea I felt so much better and by the time I stood on dry land I was well. I met Gerry and we went out for a drink.

One evening we were invited to the Empire Gull for a Chinese New Year Party.

The crew were all Chinese and they provided us a real Chinese meal to celebrate the occasion.

We started with bird nest soup but when I heard what was in it, it put me right of drinking it.

Next loads of dishes were put on the table and we helped ourselves. I loved the prawns but the black things I thought were mushrooms turned out to be 100 day eggs. I love Indian cuisine but I'm not very fond of Chinese cooking but the guests, who did, thoroughly enjoyed themselves.

The best part of the meal was the taste of the cocoa we had before leaving the ship.

We were invited to cocktail parties at Khormaksar mess and they were usually held outside where the lovely evenings made the event very pleasurable.

One evening as we joked with a group of men one remarked to Maggie "I'm glad I haven't got a child in your class."

Now Maggie, a Scots girl from Fraser burgh (second cave on the left after Aberdeen was the address she always gave) was a very good teacher with excellent references and results who usually taught the 11 year olds. Another officer standing by rounded on the speaker and said, "If you had a child in her class she would be very lucky indeed." Maggie eventually ended up as a head in a Kings X School.

As we chatted an officer who had only just arrived from UK asked me what I did. I replied I was a mistress in the Officers' Mess.

He smiled and he had obviously noted I wasn't wearing a wedding ring so said "Are you a nurse?"

I replied "No I am a mistress in the Officers' Mess."

He turned to a Wing Commander standing next and asked him if he knew what I did. The WC who had been listening to our conversation said with a very straight face, "She's a mistress in the Officers Mess."

The newcomer was almost convinced but asked how I had got the job as he hadn't heard of anything like this before.

Truthfully I said, "I went to the Air Ministry for an interview and they gave me the job."

By this time he was convinced and he asked if he could avail himself of my services that night. I said he could but not that night as I had the CO and he booked me for the night. Now that was a lie.

I told him he could make an appointment if he came to the billiard room at 10 am the next morning when I took my bookings. We moved on and I forgot all about our conversation.

Next morning at 10 am I was in front of my class. I was sitting at my high desk and the children were in their desks in front of me all hard at work. Then a head popped round the door. He had arrived to make an appointment and it obviously took him a few minutes to take in the situation. His eyes widened and he looked quite miffed then disappeared. I never saw him again. I was surprised he hadn't discussed it with other officers in the mess but if he had they had gone along with the joke and would have teased him unmercifully.

I had a letter from my army postal friend to say they were evacuating Agaba and moving to Cyprus and they would be travelling via Aden. It seemed a long way round to me but I suppose the boat they were catching was on its way to Aden and they could then fly from Aden to Cyprus.

I arranged to meet him and take him to Gold Mohur for a swim. I arrived at Khomaska at the appointed time and two men walked out to meet me. I hadn't a clue which one was Ken until he spoke. He had brought his friend and they piled into my little car, one in front and one squashed into the ledge at the back.

We had a pleasant day at Gold Mohur and they told me they would be a few days in Aden until transport arrived. The few days lengthened into weeks and Ken and I went out often to restaurants and dances. We had a date one Saturday night and in our mess at lunch time Mac said "Oh your postie was on the phone, he can't meet you as he's been posted to Cyprus."

Saturday night and I had been stood up. He didn't write and I didn't know his address so I forgot about him and found someone else

A few days later in our mess Mac again met me with, "Your postie has been on the phone and he's been posted to Aden and he's staying at Tarshyne, he'll contact you later."

I had met an oil man Ivan Little in Aden and he invited me to a dance. It was about 20 miles away and I wasn't keen on travelling back alone late at night. He offered to put me up in his quarters. All the oil personnel had very nice homes and his was no exception but as I didn't know him all that well I was doubtful about accepting his offer. As it happened Maggie also got an invitation to the dance so that meant we could come back to our own flat.

The dance ended late and we set off home, we were about half way back when the engine began to splutter and the speed dropped until we were just crawling along. I was loath to stop because we didn't know who was around and I wouldn't have known what to do if I'd looked at the engine. We came to a village and crawled through that hoping no one would approach us. We got through and eventually reached Khormaksar beach and home. We were a little shaken but all's well that ends well.

Ken contacted me and we carried on where we had left off.

We decided we'd better have a warming party so once we were settled we invited our friends, and other teachers from the secondary school who also had a flat on the beach. They invited their friends so there was a mixed bunch many of whom we had never met. We had to have a theme for the event and the rage at that time was for pyjama parties so that was the theme we adopted.

Everyone fell in with the plan and the evening our guests arrived wearing various types of pyjamas. I had recently acquired some "baby doll" pyjamas with ribbons and bows and blue hearts painted on a white background. They were short, the trousers finished just below the knee and they were fetching. No I didn't wear them. Ken did and very nice he looked too. His friend Fred arrived and he looked gorgeous. He wore a nightie, a shortie which I think he got from Maggie. With his blue eyes and tight blond curls he was very glamorous.

The party was a success, plenty of booze and eats. We didn't bother the neighbours as they too were having a party but there's was very 'posh' – dinner jackets and black ties.

As the evening progressed the two parties observed each other from the balconies and eventually our 'thrash' decided to invade the posh do. They formed a conga and sang and danced their way through the neighbours flat. Their guests joined the merriment – and the conga so this motley line wended its way through the flats, evening dresses and pyjamas evenly spaced.

Fred had acquired a paper streamer from the decorations and tucked an end in his underpants as one lady in evening dress passed him, he grabbed her, sat her on his knee, lifted his nightie and waving the streamer said "Have you ever seen a coloured one?"

It was quite a party and when eventually the crowds had gone we tidied up a bit. Ken then decided he should go but couldn't find his clothes. The keys for his car were in his trousers so he was in a quandary.

Fortunately Fred's mess was on the beach quite close by and Fred had a scooter. Ken walked in his baby doll pyjamas to Fred's but Fred was fast asleep and in the nuddy snoring away.

Ken covered up the ghastly sight with an eiderdown which was on the floor, collected the keys and drove to Tarshyne at the other end of Aden.

Next day he returned the scooter and Fred was leaning on the gate rather the worse for wear. "So that's where the scooter went – and I suppose you threw the eiderdown over me?" He had woken in the night roasting hot, drenched with perspiration.

They arrived at our flat a little later to help with the final clearing up and I told Ken I had found his clothes neatly folded beneath my pillow. We never knew who had put them there but we all agreed it had been a good party.

A week later at Gold Mohur we were chatting with some BOAC personnel who were saying that in the next block of flats on the beach had been a party. It had been very noisy and many of the people were wearing pyjamas. They inferred that there had been some queer goings on and had we heard about it. We feigned ignorance but were amazed how rumours spread so quickly in a small community.

We did our shopping in the local shops and markets either in Aden or Crater which was a short distance inland through a pass and into what had been a volcanic crater now extinct at least we hoped so. One of the teachers, Kevin, had an apartment there and we often called for a cold drink if we were in the vicinity.

My little Fiat was a wonderful little run about and I don't think we could have managed without it. The buses didn't come to the beach and there were no telephone for us to contact taxis. Maggie bought a Topolino but she hadn't passed her test in UK. Although she was issued with a licence in Aden she wasn't very competent and lacked confidence. Her car was usually driven by the current boyfriend.

Maggie and I did most of the shopping and in the Crater market one morning the shop keeper told us our mother was very lucky. We didn't understand what he meant and in his broken English he explained "Because she has two girls the same age." He thought we were twins. We probably all looked alike to him.

All the people we met in Aden were lovely. They always seemed so friendly and happy and we were quite happy to wonder the streets either alone or in a group.

Naturally in Aden we were quickly known as locals as we were always in the shops. The chemist in particular welcomed our visits and we bought perfumes and cosmetics etc. and he always gave us free samples from under the counter even when we bought nothing.

We got wise to the fact that we never shopped when a passenger liner was in port. The first time we tried the shop keeper drew us to one side and shook his head and pointed to tourists. We realised when they were in town the prices rocketed. Even then they were very cheap by British Standards but we got better prices when they were not around.

It was about this time that we noticed the short skirts on the women passengers. We were still wearing the New Look, 1947 calf length skirts and here were women with skirts just below the knees. They looked so funny and out of place but by the time we were coming back to UK we were the funny and out of place women.

One of our friends and a regular visitor to the flats was Bonnie. She was a SAAFA sister and apart from helping doctors she went round the area checking on sick people and checking that babies were well cared for and making the necessary progress. After a hard morning's work she often arrived at the flat ad had a gin and tonic.

The tumbler was half filled with gin and after a few sips the tonic would be put in. Fortunately she had a driver so the roads were quite safe. Not so some of her patients. As the doctor was Catholic she was left to fit the women with contraceptive devices.

She wasn't very good because if the women returned and they complained of pain she knew it was too big but if it slipped out she knew it was too small. I think she was joking, but when I remarked that many women could become pregnant unexpectedly she said she was going home in a few weeks so wouldn't know the outcome. However the long arm of the Medie RAF would always find her so I'm sure she really was joking.

Before she went however we went on a holiday to Kenya. I had been before but that was only a weekend in Mombasa. This was a few days in Nairobi and a few days in Mombasa. She had only one week but I had decided to have ten days holiday.

We travelled with Eagle Airways who still had the contract to fly forces personnel to East Africa.

We had a lovely hotel in Nairobi and visited all the sights including a tour of the Safari Park.

We saw all the usual animals and it was fascinating to see them so close. They ignored us completely and even seemed bored by the close proximity of excited visitors taking so many photographs and cine pictures. Of course we were in vehicles but at one point we got out near a river. The guards pointed out a crocodile sunning himself on the opposite bank. He looked quite harmless but had it crept out of the long grass near where we stood we would have been terrified.

I judged I could outrun him back to our vehicle if he made an effort to cross the river.

As it was August it was Kenya's winter and the nights were cold. At one point I wrapped my legs in newspaper as I lay in bed and shivered with cold. Even Yorkshire winters hadn't felt so cold but then I had had a hot water bottle. So I was very glad when we got on the train to Mombasa. We had the compartment to ourselves, it was very comfortable and the sun was shining.

The views were magnificent, as they say, "Miles and miles of bloody Africa", and it was beautiful. The only blight on the journey was as we were nearing Mombasa the train slowed right down and then stopped. We looked out of the window and a dead body was on the line. I don't know what happened but it was the first dead person I had ever seen it was not very pleasant.

Mombasa was lovely and warm, not as hot and humid as Aden but much better than Nairobi and Bonnie and I relaxed. We had had dinner in our hotel and we had got chatting to two men. They were going to Malindi – a place on the coast, and offered to take us out for dinner and show us round. They had a business to do with aeroplanes and were expecting a delivery from America. Apparently it arrived in kit form and once assembled it had to be tested.

We were on the airfield as John made the test flight and everything seemed to be in order. They were going to Malindi for the weekend and he suggested we went with them. Unfortunately Bonnie was returning to Aden and I didn't really want to go on my own with them. Bonnie said I was being stupid and John would hardly be planning to seduce me and taking his brother along.

So I decided to go, so in the newly assembled plane which could only hold six passengers we set off. I sat in the front with John the pilot and he pointed out all the places of interest in the area as we flew to the holiday resort of Malindi.

As we approached John started to do 'tricks' with the plane, stalling it and diving etc. I was terrified and screamed and when he had finished playing around he said, "Jean, you were never in any danger because my life is more precious to me than yours."

Malindi as far as I could see consisted of one hotel and few shambas nearby. It was a holiday place for the white residents of Kenya and virtually unknown to tourists.

So it was quite an occasion when I wandered into the restaurant with the two brothers and you could almost see and hear everyone saying "Who's that and where did they get her from?"

I think John and his brother derived great pleasure from providing the holiday makers with a mystery because after all everyone in Kenya knew everyone else. If they bothered to look at the registration book they would be even more intrigued to see a name with Aden as the place of my residence.

It was a lovely weekend even if it did rain for much of the time and I returned to Aden refreshed and ready for work – and play.

My little car was a treasure. It was easy to drive, climbed the hill to Crater without any bother, of course it had to do so in a lower gear, but nevertheless it got me wherever I wanted to go. I really don't know how we would have managed as Khomaksar beach was off the beaten track. I drove it all over and ferried friends and collected shopping. Since I passed my test – 1948 (first time!) I had driven all over England including the lakes, and of course Cyprus and I had never had an accident.

And then getting petrol at one of the stations a car drove in front of me so I reversed to get out and bumped the car behind. The owner was speechless. He could only point at the damage on his vehicle which happened to be a dent in his front bumper. My little car hadn't a scratch. I apologised and said I had looked behind when the way was clear but the other motorist had pulled in front of me and reversed without another glance. As it was private property I didn't think it had to be reported and he agreed he'd get another bumper and I would pay. And that was that – or was it?

For the next few days I worried and thought if he had the bumper sent Air mail I would be in for quite a hefty payment. Eventually I went to Mr Rice my headmaster and explained what had happened. He was an old hand in Aden and that night he was having dinner with the Chief of Police and he said he would put my case to him.

Next day he told me virtually to pay up and look pleasant. Apparently an accident has to be reported immediately and if it isn't the perpetrator could even go to jail; an Aden jail? Not likely, I paid the price of the bumper and it wasn't exorbitant so I felt that was the end of the matter.

I could understand the annoyance of the owner of the bumped car because it was brand new. Many people bought cars when they were in Aden as they were cheap and provided you had it for a year before you returned to UK you didn't have to pay tax. In fact one of the members of our civilian mess bought a Mercedes and kept it in the show room but brought it out each Saturday. He drove it to little Aden and back quite a few times to get mileage on the clock and then put it back in the showroom.

He would ask people during the week – "Do you want a twirl in my motor on Saturday?" He liked the company as it was a bit boring driving up and down the same road on your own.

The reason he was taking great care of his car was because it was a Mercedes. His brother was a well-known and popular Scottish singer and he only had a Cortina and Mac wanted to drive up in his lovely Mercedes and surprise him and gloat.

Mr Rice's wife was still in England so I suppose he was quite lonely living on his own in a hiring. We invited him to a curry party and after everyone had gone he helped us prepare the evening meal. We gave him the potatoes to peel but that was a mistake as most of the potato came off with the skin but he had had a few drinks!

To reciprocate he invited Ken and me to a meal at his home and on our arrival he gave us each a drink and after a while said he'd better go to see how the dinner was coming on then disappeared into the kitchen and after a while called us into the dining room for dinner. We ate the best delicious spaghetti bolognaise followed by pizza and coffee. I was annoyed that a 'mere' man could produce such a meal and told him his wife had trained him well.

It wasn't until after weeks later he told us his secret. He had an arrangement with an Italian restaurant in Aden whereby he gave them the order of food which had to be ready on the counter when he arrived to pick it up. Whilst he was in the kitchen 'seeing to the food' he raced down to the restaurant picked up his order and served it as his own cooking. It was obviously a split second operation but he amazed many of his guests with his 'culinary expertise.'

After two terms with my class the Officers' Mess numbers fell and I moved back into the school buildings. No longer was I a mistress in the Officers' Mess. Mr Rice also moved me to an A class as he felt I had had enough time with children who needed extra help.

Later in the year we had a HMI inspection. Two men came out from England and stayed in the Rock Hotel. They spent a week with us and visited the school from Assembly to home time. They moved from class to class at will so we had no idea when they would be in our rooms. Each closing time they took sets of books with them and went through them in the evenings. At the end of the week they gave a report to Mr Rice and then moved to Kenya to inspect the Forces' schools there. At least by the time they left us they were not so white and had managed to get their knees a little brown.

Their official report from UK was excellent and why not? Apart from dedicated and good teaching we had a wonderful set of children. I can't remember ever having to shout or smack (it was allowed in those days) any of them. I don't remember any other teacher doing so. I wonder if the discipline their fathers had in the RAF rubbed off on the children. I certainly can't say the same for my civilian classes.

Maggie had got friendly with a few army types and one of them had married a Richmond girl who turned out to be a friend of mine. Of course Richmond was a small market town so everyone knew everyone else. She also met up with a friend of her cousin who said he was a dab hand at curry making so we decided to have a curry lunch. Bill told us what he needed in way of ingredients so on Saturday morning we bought all the stuff plus the liquid intake we would need and to set to work to concoct his masterpiece. During the preparation and cooking he regaled us with his songs which became more risqué with each pint he consumed. I seem to remember we started off with 'On the banks of Moya River' and progressed to 'He's got the biggest and the best in Africa; it really is a lovely sight – the biggest and the best is a water melon!' We also had 'My rhubarb refused to rise,' and we had a lovely morning cooking and singing. As with all our parties where food was consumed the cooks or cocktail mixer could have as much to drink as they liked on preparation day but had to remain fairly sober on party day.

Sunday morning our guests arrived and Bill's curry lived up to his promises. All the dishes were delicious. He had made a few different types and had come in early on Sunday morning to do all the side dishes.

In Aden each mess vied with the other to produce curry lunch but that day Bills excelled them all.

Three young ladies living on their own in a flat on a beach could have been at risk but we were opposite a hospital and there were other blocks of flats nearby. However at night I suppose we were fairly vulnerable. This never occurred to us until one particular night. There had been a very strong wind and a few days previously the front door had slammed breaking the glass in the top half leaving a rather large space.

In the middle of the night there was a loud knocking on the door and I seemed to be the only one to hear it or at least to get up and investigate. Fortunately I had the presence of mind to ask who it was before I opened the door. "I got a very rude response," came the reply and I stood rooted to the spot.

Young ladies weren't used to language like that in those days. I yelled! Maggie, Maggie, Joan, Joan and eventually they both arrived wondering what on earth the matter was. When I explained we opened the door but of course there was no one there.

We told our respective boyfriends and the only explanation put forward and I must admit I find it hard to believe, was that drivers occasionally dropped Maggie's and Joan's boyfriends at the flat after they had been flying and would know we lived there alone and perhaps had told others. We had a good laugh as no damage had been done but we had the glass replaced very quickly.

At one time there was trouble from various factions in the Yemen. We never knew what led to trouble as we always had the utmost respect and friendship from local people with whom we had contact.

But the RAF rounded up many Arabs and they were put behind barbed wire in a compound and guarded. We could see them as we went to school but we knew little of what was going on.

When the crisis had passed the internees were taken in lorries to the beach and released. We happened to be sitting on the balcony enjoying the evening sunshine when the lorries drew up outside our flat. The men were released and ran up the beach towards Sheikh Othmen. Then the buses, and there were quite a few, drove away.

A far as we knew none of the 'prisoners' doubled back but we thought it strange releasing en masse men who had been in custody for weeks outside a residential area.

Many of the forces abroad bought cars and as long as they kept them a year they could take them back to UK and avoid paying tax. If someone went on leave during that year they usually left the car in charge of a friend and that's how Kevin, one of our staff came to be in charge of a Vauxhall car.

He was also looking after the car owner's dogs so he needed the car to take the dogs to the beach and that's how he came to Khomaksar on a certain day when the tide was at its lowest for the year; a leap tide I believe it is called. He was driving the car close to the water when it stopped. We don't know why it stopped but it was at the edge of the water at low tide on the finest tide of the year.

He dashed to our flat which was close by knowing Ken and Fred could possibly be there. In any case, if they weren't the REME Mess where Fred lived was close by so he could dash there to get help. Ken or Fred was in and we all dashed to the beach to see what had happened. By the time we reached it the tide had turned and was already up to the hubs on the wheels. Two Arabs had come to help and they were frantically digging the sand at the wheels to try to release them but as fast as they dug the tide deposited more sand in the holes they had made.

We all tried to do something but Mother Nature defeated every effort and within a short time the car was covered by the water and firmly embedded in the sand.

Fred, an engineer with a science degree seized the opportunity to give his lads a practical exercise using the machinery available to the Army. With permission from a senior officer and all the equipment and men necessary we all assembled 24 hours later. Mr Rice and other teachers were all there to witness the 'fun' and join in the rescue.

Fred had obtained a Scammell which had a hawser to attach to the car and pull it free – in theory. By this time the car had sand inside up to the dashboard and after much debate it was decided to attach the hawser to the metal between the windows on the far side. Eventually the windows were opened, the Scammell attached and Fred ordered his men to pull the hawser in. The rope stretched and took the strain. It tightened and the car roof dented but the car itself didn't move.

Again the lads controlled the machine and gently the rope tightened even more and with a metal grating sound a sudden upward swoop the whole roof bent up into the air.

It was such an anti-climax and everyone after a deathly pause burst into laughter. The car was a write off and no further attempt was made to free it.

The REME had had something different to do and we had enjoyed the interlude but Kevin had to face the wrath of the owners if they ever returned.

The sequel to this was, a few months later Maggie came into my room at school and said "Look at this." One of the children in her diary about what she had been doing at the weekend had written "We were on the Khormaksur beach and found the ruin of a car at the water's edge" I wonder if it's still there!

Maggie had a cousin who was married to a man who was a manager in the cigarette factory in Jinga Uganda. In 1958 we decided to go for our summer holiday to visit the family. To get there we first had to fly to Nairobi with Eagle Airways Ken had fixed us up to stay with the major who was in charge of the Postal Services in the Middle East. He had a very nice bungalow at Kabete a few miles out of Nairobi where he lived with his Austrian wife and three children.

We knew Don the Major quite well as on his visits to Aden to inspect the postal service his favourite mess was ours, the civilian officer's mess at Ma'alla. We all spent some happy evenings there and Don was definitely a party animal. He was full of fun and great company, whenever I drove him in my little Fiat and we passed Ma'alla Mess he would stand up and take the salute.

We spent a couple of nights until we booked a passage on the overnight train to Uganda where we would be met by Maggie's cousin.

The trains were very comfortable and it was lovely waking up next morning to the different scenery. Maggie's cousin had arranged a party on the Saturday night, after all there was a shortage of women so two new ones would be quite exciting. She was planning the food and wondered if we knew any good recipes for desserts as everyone on the party circuit was sick of the same things. We didn't.

I decided not to stay in Uganda but return to Nairobi to stay with Don and family. Don sent this telegram to Ken in Aden.

Subject Person Effect (1)

Your baggage from Jinja now to hand at Nairobi (1)

Should this be forwarded to you or will you collect (1)

Urgent reply appreciated////

18th August 1958.

When Ken received it he took leave and caught a plane to Nairobi.

We had a lovely few days. We went to the Outspan Hotel where Princess Elizabeth was told she had become Queen Elizabeth and I had the most beautiful room in the hotel but Ken had to do with a shamba hut in grounds of the Hotel. It wasn't the thing in those days to share holiday accommodation if you weren't married.

We returned to Aden and I suppose it took us three quarters of an hour to get to the flat and Ken was already complaining about the heat. I said "Feel my feet." They were still cold after all August in Kenya is the middle of winter and although not like a winter in UK it was certainly colder than in Aden.

Ken had to go to Bahrain and I think whilst he was away he decided to ask me to marry him. On his return we went to dinner at the Richigee Carigee Galleon Grill and as I dropped him off at the Steamer Point Officers Mess he popped the question with the proviso that he would have to be earning £1000 a year in civilian life. He was seconded to the army from the civil service and although he had been promoted to HEO 'in absentia' he felt the pay wasn't quite enough in which to keep a wife.

Well if he wasn't all that keen to make a decision and marriage depended on money it didn't seem right to procrastinate so I said either he wanted to marry me or he didn't. He decided he did, but first I would finish my contract which expired at Easter. Ken was returning to the UK in November and thought he might be posted to Germany so we thought we might get married there on my return.

Maggie and I had been shopping in Aden and driving back to the flat she asked me if I was going to marry Ken. I replied I hadn't thought about it and she said, "Well you obviously get on well together," and I realised he made me laugh and I did enjoy being with him and my life had altered since we met in Aden.

So in November Ken left for the UK and I stayed to finish my contract with the RAF.

Fred took over from Ken and as Christmas was approaching we went to parties and dances together and thoroughly enjoyed ourselves.

Christmas 1958 came and there were the usual parties and for Christmas dinner we decided to invite our friends to dinner which we would cook. So there were eight of us. Joy and her boyfriend, Maggie and John and Fred and I.

Our deputy head was on his own as his wife had returned to the UK as she was expecting a baby and also to settle at home as he was due back in January. John had an old friend who was on his own so he asked if he could bring him so we settled down to a turkey dinner.

Usually I did the cooking as Maggie found the kitchen too hot and in fact I have seen the perspiration dripping off her hair when she has offered to help. We found the arrangement worked well, she oversaw to the cleaning and I cooked, Joyce did her own thing with her boyfriend.

So eight of us sat down to a huge turkey and trimmings and even though I say it myself, it was good.

After the Christmas pudding and the coffee and mince pies and liqueurs we sat on the balcony and chatted and relaxed.

After about two hours John said "What are you going to do with the rest of the turkey?"

"Well we'll have it for lunch tomorrow I suppose, why?"

"It seems a shame to keep it in the fridge." He replied. Now John had a prodigious appetite and was known to clear everyone else's plates if they couldn't manage it for themselves.

"Surely you can't eat anymore?" said his friend.

It was obvious he could, so we said "Go and get what you want."

He went into the kitchen and emerged with the carcass, put it on the table and began to pick at it, we all derided him, but eventually his friend went to sit at the table. Fred followed and then our deputy head and before long we were all sitting round the table, eating turkey and drinking wine.

We didn't have any turkey next day!

Years later we were staying with John in Cornwall and he took us to his local pub. John steered the conversation to Aden and one of his friends said he had been stationed there and had had a Christmas dinner with some teachers and friends.

It was the same friend John had brought to the flat and he had wanted to see my reaction when I realised who he was.

Fred continued to take me out to all the Christmas parties, Ken sent me an engagement ring so people who didn't know us would think I was engaged to Fred. One night in Ma'alla Civilian Officers' Mess Fred and I were having a friendly discussion – well, argument and a man standing next to us said, "If she's like that when you are engaged what is she going to be like when you marry?"

We both turned on him and said "We're not marrying each other." He must have thought it a funny set up but this was Aden and it was a bit like Kenya with the adage "Are you married or do you live in Kenya?"

With only one more term to do until my return to UK Mr Rice then had approached me and said "Normally I would ask you to be Deputy Head but as you are getting married would you mind if I offered it to Maggie as it will do more for her career." Well it certainly wasn't worth while being a DH for one term and in any case my thoughts wouldn't be on the job so naturally I agreed with him.

It certainly helped Maggie in her career as she went on to be a Head of a London School and I returned at Easter to UK.

Eagle Airways flew me back and as I knew the crew I got chatting to them.

"They'll sting you at customs," I was told. "Everyone who comes from Aden no matter who they are, is charged duty."

I had never been charged duty on any of my return trips to UK but this was different.

I was asked by the Customs officer if I had plenty of money on me. "You don't charge duty on cash do you?" I asked.

"No but you'll have plenty to pay on this lot."

"But many of the things are wedding presents and I understand they are duty free."

I had to pay on a watch, a cine camera and various other items although he did allow me to bring in free a clock Maggie had given me for a wedding present.

Everyone paid duty on everything if they were coming from Aden.

Ken met me at the Airport and no longer was I a mistress abroad.

THE END